BUILDINGS *of the* YEAR

The RIBA architecture awards

Tony Chapman

RIBA ₥ **Publishing**

Text © Royal Institute of British Architects, 2012
Photographs © the photographers and architects
(see individual projects)

Published by RIBA Publishing,
15 Bonhill Street, London EC2P 2EA

ISBN 978 1 85946 490 8

Stock code 79287

British Library Cataloguing in Publications Data
A catalogue record for this book is available from the
British Library.

Commissioning Editor: Steven Cross
Picture Researcher: Clemency Christopherson
Project Editor: Alex Lazarou
Book Designer: Alex Lazarou
Printed and bound in Great Britain by
Butler Tanner & Dennis, Frome and London, UK

RIBA Publishing is part of RIBA Enterprises Ltd.
www.ribaenterprises.com

What are awards for?

Tony Chapman
HON FRIBA

ASK AN AWARD-WINNING ARCHITECT what awards are for and they'll tell you they're a reward for good work done in the face of adversity, which often comes in the shape of indecisive, mean clients; planners whose mental clocks are set to 1907, or if you're lucky 1957; and contractors who tut-tut, 'it can't be done mate, can't be done'.

Ask a less good architect (yes, there are good and not so – that's what awards are primarily about in fact – separating the one from t'other), one who's probably never entered a decent building into a decent award scheme, let alone won a prize, and they'll tell you they're made by a bunch of elitist architects in London as part of an exercise in mutual back-scratching and if you live outside the M25 you might as well not bother entering.

Ask the public what awards are for and they'll either say, 'sorry?' or that they reflect the personal tastes (or hates) of the Prince of Wales, Kevin McCloud or the President of the RIBA.

Ask a journalist and they'll rewrite the question and tell you what you should be asking is, 'what do awards prove?' This is probably the most misguided response as awards don't *prove* anything, they don't *do* things, they *are* what the architectural process demands, otherwise there would be no point in sending judges to visit the buildings; the winners could be determined by committee according to their pre-set agenda and an exercise in box ticking. The RIBA has been told constantly this year what *should* be on the Stirling shortlist in order to make this point or that. They just don't get it. The shortlist exists for one purpose only: what is – within the 730 of those submitted – the best building in the European Union by an RIBA chartered architect.

Journalists also ask whether there's a pattern, or a theme, in a shortlist? If asked this I reply, 'I leave that to you'. Finding patterns is what journalists do (I know, I used to be one); it is not the job of an organiser of architectural awards. Most things can be post-rationalised – although there should be a prize equivalent to the monetary value of the Stirling Prize itself, for whoever could find a meaningful pattern in a stadium, a cancer centre, a theatre, a laboratory, a gallery and a bank. A bank? Who in their right mind these days would deliberately choose to put a bank on a shortlist for any other reason but excellence? Because that is what all these buildings have in common: they're all bloody good.

'OK then', the journalist comes back, feet dancing like a boxer's, 'why do these lists always contain the well-known suspects?' Like coppers pulling in the same old villains every time some OAP gets coshed or a bank gets robbed. 'Come on Norman, you've got form.' 'Why me? I've been clean since 2004. I ain't been anywhere near Stirling since then.'

Awards are a meritocracy. You get them because you deserve to. At the risk of going all Michael Gove, competing is important but winning is what really matters. It is in order to replicate this pyramid of achievement

Lyric Theatre
IMAGE: DENNIS GILBERT

Hepworth Wakefield
IMAGE: HUFTON + CROW

that this year we have re-organised the RIBA awards programme. It has taken the best part of two years – not that far short of what it took to get the Olympics agreed – to get the changes through a variety of RIBA committees. In fact the RIBA Awards *are* a bit like the Olympics. You train (as an athlete or architect), you enter trials/competitions, you compete, you're selected and you build your performance/building. You enter the Olympics/the Awards; there are heats/shortlisting, you win through, there are semi-finals/midlisting; you're in the final/on the Stirling shortlist; from hundreds you're down to the final few. At which point, for an architect, it becomes more like gymnastics or diving than track events: artistic impression is more important than being on time or even on budget. What it certainly is not like is synchronised swimming or beach volleyball, as this is *not* a beauty contest. Building a legacy is as important as short term success.

But to begin again at the beginning. The RIBA Awards have been going since 1966, the year of the Beach Boys' *Pet Sounds* and the Beatles' *Revolver*, the year before the summer of love, to put them in their cultural context. Odd that in such a time, an aspirationally egalitarian time, that the RIBA should be launching such a competitive initiative.

Or maybe not. This was also the decade Prime Minister Wilson's white heat of technology was to be our saviour, along with comprehensives and the Open University. And anyway, the RIBA Awards were never that elitist, there was no one winner, all were equal. Only gradually did it dawn on people that clearly that was not the case. So along came National Awards – a handful, all equal. And finally the Building of the Year, hand picked by the RIBA President – how elitist was that? So the Stirling Prize, when it was invented at the fin de siècle, with Tony Blair surfing the crest of a wave that would surge him into Downing Street, was relatively democratic and very much of its time. So much did it appeal to Blair that, having sent along his cohorts Chris Smith and Peter Mandelson to present the early prizes, he threatened to put in an appearance himself in 2000. An even more pressing engagement ended up saving him from having to witness winner Will Alsop's expletive-laden frustration with the planners of Kensington and Chelsea and being kept waiting for his dinner by the agents of Channel 4, struggling to televise the prize for the first time. But I digress.

Peckham Library
IMAGE: RODERICK COYNE

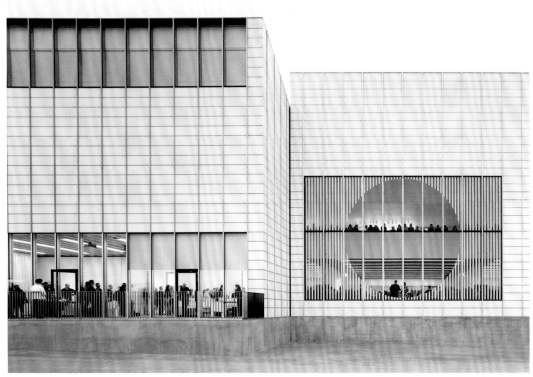

Turner Contemporary
IMAGE: SIMON MENGES

In the wake of the RIBA Awards, like a flotilla of squabbling ducklings, came the regional awards. Some were heading in vaguely the same direction, some not. Some were open to all-comers, others were keen to ensure the purity of the lineage of said ducklings, insisting their progenitors were born, bred and practised in the region, while some were barren of awards altogether. Try to enter for a regional award in Mercia, or Mancunium, or Londinium (I exaggerate, but only to emphasise how jealously regions guarded – or denied – their heritage), and you'd be met with blank stares. Then there was the matter of chronology. Some presented their awards after Stirling – whether this was admirable or just cute depended on your point of view or postcode. Either way, it was confusing, as was the need to enter projects to the same institution for an award twice and pay two fees. Not to mention wasteful of architects' and organisers' time. Maybe it took a Yorkshireman to deracinate the White Rose Awards, but at the same time I tore down Hadrian's walls and laid waste town and country. Or so those regions who ran awards with those names feared. In fact I didn't, I made sure all this heritage survived. (I wasn't a judge for the Crown Estate Conservation Award all those years for nothing.)

The new system allows for cakes to be eaten and had: a simpler, logical, more rigorous pyramid of awards built on local foundations. Things aren't perfect, but then it took 47 years to get it wrong and we won't get it exactly right in year one. Year two maybe. What's more, all of this makes little or no difference to Stirling, although it is having a beneficial impact on the Stephen Lawrence Prize and the RIBA Manser Medal, giving them rather more small projects or houses to choose their shortlists from, regional as well as RIBA Awards. Of the former there are naturally far more than there used to be, of the latter there are fewer, restoring the value of an RIBA Award to what it was ten years ago: a beneficial by-product.

So after all this, are we any clearer about what architectural awards are for? I think we are. They're to point up what's good, and implicitly less good, about what architects do, and to shout about it from the rooftops. Simple really. Even if it does take 70 people three quarters of the year to do it. Here endeth the first lesson.

Dellow Day Centre
IMAGE: TIM BROTHERTON

Opening doors to good architecture

Angela Brady

RIBA PRESIDENT

IAM A FIRM BELIEVER that architects should be seen and heard. Words are not always an architect's forte, but if we are to affirm the power of our collective voice as leaders of the construction industry, we need to speak out clearly and consistently in both public and policymaking contexts. So whenever I am offered a platform (and sometimes when I'm not), I speak out about the need for a more simplified procurement process for public construction projects – one that benefits smaller practices – and I speak out about the many benefits that great architectural design brings to a project and to wider society.

The RIBA celebrates great clients every year with our Client of The Year (see page 90). Would that our cumbersome procurement methods allowed them all to be so good. To produce award-winning buildings we have to get the process right from the start. Awards and competitions are two sides of the same coin and well-run competitions can lead to award-winning architecture.

Most of the Olympic projects were procured through competitions. The Beatbox by Pernilla and Asif is a great example of a young team creating an exquisite project – and equal credit goes to architect Kevin Owens who headed up design for the Olympic projects. Our forthcoming film *Designing for Champions* will show just how good the other 51 schemes were.

The RIBA has supported the principle of architectural competitions since 1871, and a century later set up a permanent competitions unit based in Leeds. Today, the institute is the UK's most widely recognised organisation, with the expertise and experience to support the process from the initial client idea through to project commission and completion.

Architectural competitions help practices win business and showcase creativity. They are also a highly successful procurement model that brings out the best in a project – often giving a platform to new and emerging talent.

Through our RIBA members, the unit also has access to top-class, highly-skilled and impartial assessors to help clients prepare the right brief and judge the entries. The role of the RIBA architect adviser is core and exclusive to this service, and highly valued by clients. In these difficult times for procurement, running efficient, well-briefed competitions is one way to help prioritise good design.

Design competitions benefit architects and clients alike. Running more competitions could help put design excellence top of the agenda. Kay Hughes, formerly from the Olympic Delivery Authority (ODA), which saw many of the 2012 projects designed this way, has said: 'A competition brings in the highest quality of thinking to your project, and as a client it gives you the best range of options to choose from.'

Primary substation for 2012 Olympics
IMAGE: ANDREW LEE

Some of the most striking buildings and design projects across the UK are the result of competitions, from Blackpool Wind Shelters (Ian McChesney) to affordable inner-city housing such as Iroko at London's Coin Street by Haworth Tompkins. Former Guardian architecture critic Jonathan Glancey said of it: 'The buildings really are exceptional by any local authority, housing association or housing charity standards – a breath of fresh air in polluted inner London.'

Ricky Burdett of the London School of Economics worked with Richard Rogers on the London Plan and with the ODA promoted competitions. The most important achievement was to get the London Development Agency and Transport for London to accept that 'design quality' should be a major and not secondary criterion, and that design professionals and not just project managers should be involved in making that assessment. He believes the key elements for a design competition include a good brief with a clear vision, a good jury containing a majority of design professionals, and a good client (or one well-advised by design experts).

Burdett advises allowing enough time to understand the site and develop the brief, and to let design teams gear up, put together the right team and think of the right solution. Clients should be realistic about how much each team will actually spend (often far more than the fee). Where possible, the competition process should be used for client and design teams to get to know each other through workshops, rather than decisions made relying on amazing images to wow at the very end. He cites Tate Modern as an example of a well-run competition. A two-stage process led to a shortlist of 13, followed by six design workshops between Tate staff and design teams, which were critical to understanding the problem and finding the right team.

As chief adviser on architecture and urbanism at the ODA, Burdett was involved with many competitions. Key RIBA competition success stories are Nord's RIBA award-winning Substation, Wilkinson Eyre's Basketball Stadium and Hopkins's Stirling shortlisted Velodrome (even though the firm had never designed one before – something most clients would instinctively shy away from unless pushed by the competition process). Furthermore, the client for their Evelina Children's Hospital agrees the competition brought them the best possible building too.

Burdett advises clients not to focus too much on track records and professional indemnity levels, and to avoid being insular and risk-averse. He argues that we need to change client culture to encourage more paid competitions, especially in the public sector and make clear that design is part of the long-term investment, not an add-on. The RIBA ran 224 competitions between 2000 and 2011, 80% of which had a post-project commitment to proceed to build.

Some of the results have been stunning. Over the past nine years, 57% of projects built as a result of an RIBA competition have won design awards. Even just entering competitions helps practices build their profile and puts them in the limelight with both the public and their peers, improving access to potential clients.

Competitions can also boost innovation and creativity, which helps develop strong teams and partnerships. Niall McLaughlin says, 'Winning an RIBA competition in 2006 for Deal Pier Cafe Bar, Kent offered us the opportunity to create a type of building which the practice hadn't done before.' The pier went on to win an RIBA Award.

Competitions centre on the client's needs and the brief can require redefining, which is where an RIBA client adviser comes in. Feedback suggests the winning result often comes in above expectations, with a more innovative design than would be achieved by pre-selecting a firm based on price alone.

Urban Splash has been involved in more than ten competition projects with the RIBA. Nick Johnson, its chief executive says, 'We have produced some of our best buildings through competitions and partnering with the RIBA is an integral part of that success.' Roger Madelin of Argent, client for the King's Cross development, believes competitions bring out the best designs and lets the client choose great teams to work with. Grosvenor too, much-admired for its Stirling-shortlisted Liverpool One, commissions quality designs through competitions, which include small- and medium-sized firms on its shortlists. The success of these three clients has led to them to being elected RIBA Clients of the Year.

Liverpool Masterplan
IMAGE: PAUL MCMULLIN

Competitions make up only a fraction of the cost of a completed scheme and this investment is fundamental to securing the right team for the job, still more so when clients are relatively inexperienced. There is inevitably a fine balance for the RIBA to strike in supporting both clients and competing practices. Some clients fear that competitions cost too much, but in reality they are between 0.5% and 2.0% of the whole project cost. When considered against the whole-life costs of a building, the benefits of a well-briefed architectural competition can far outweigh that expense. As design consultant Wayne Hemingway says, 'I know there is a cost to involving the RIBA, but what it gives you is a brand that ensures you will attract high calibre entries.'

RIBA Competitions works closely with clients to achieve the highest possible level of prize money/honoraria for competitors within budget. Payments are extremely important, as many practices regard competitions as a core component of an overall marketing plan, as part of their professional development or when considering breaking into a new sector. And even for those who don't win there is important feedback available about their submission.

At community level the value of competitions could be growing, and they are often the foundation for new practices to start doing business locally. Both architects and potential clients could use the Localism Act to work with communities and stimulate public interest in our built environment. Architects can lead on projects and showcase designs that work with, rather than just for, communities.

As a practising architect, I speak from experience about the wasted time, energy and money spent on the current burdensome procurement process. Future procurement must be radically less bureaucratic – not least because the vital drivers of economic recovery are the smaller and medium-sized businesses which are often locked out of public construction contracts.

The RIBA set up a Procurement Reform Group, chaired by the award-winning housing architect Walter Menteth, who mobilised a strong multi-disciplinary team from across the whole of the construction industry.

The effectiveness of public procurement is vital to our economy, our environment and most importantly, for the users of buildings. We need procurement that delivers buildings of the best value and highest quality. However, our current public procurement system has not been working for some time and as there continues to be an uncertain economic climate, there are more reasons than ever to make it work. The process is both frustrating and wasteful for those bidding for, or unable to gain, access to contracts, and too often the resulting buildings are of a poor quality that costs too much money to build and run. It is important that we don't just analyse the problems of the past. We need to look to the future to see how we can improve and streamline the procurement process and strive for better outcomes. We need construction procurement which is better, leaner and greener; that discourages waste, encourages innovation and promotes a more collaborative and efficient way of working across the whole construction team.

I have made procurement my number one priority as RIBA President and see the report *Building Ladders of Opportunity* as the start of a wider conversation about policy change, particularly at the political level. I hope that this report makes a positive contribution to the ongoing debate around procurement reform and look forward to working with Government and industry to achieve our shared objectives.

The group's report was produced by means of consultation with a cross-professional forum, a process which engenders a stronger more authoritative voice for change. We do not claim to have all the answers, but we believe our solutions are achievable and can help deliver on some of the Government's key areas of ambition.

The construction industry has an annual turnover of more than £100bn and represents almost 10% of UK GDP, with some 40% of this being in the public sector. The admission implicit in current reform initiatives is that public construction procurement is expensive and inefficient, delivering buildings that are of sub-standard design quality and sustainability, in a market with significant barriers to fair access and competition.

With growth badly needed, now is the time for wholesale reform of public construction procurement. Our current economic climate makes it an imperative. I hope our recommendations will be embraced, to the benefit of the public, the public sector and the wider construction industry.

Briefly our recommendations are:
- To further examine the best ways to drive efficiencies and savings to ensure the public procurement system functions in the best interests of all those it serves.
- To embed processes that ensure buildings are sustainable by focusing on design outcomes.
- And to create a competitive market by increasing access and allowing the public sector to take full advantage of all UK design talent.

Over the coming year the RIBA will continue to work closely with the Government to embed our recommendations in the detail of procurement policy. I am also looking forward to inviting our construction colleagues back to the RIBA to continue the debate and build future partnerships. I also firmly believe architects will be all the stronger for working collaboratively with other built environment professionals – in this and other areas.

THE RIBA STIRLING PRIZE

THE WINNER

SAINSBURY LABORATORY, CAMBRIDGE
Stanton Williams

THE SHORTLIST

THE HEPWORTH WAKEFIELD
David Chipperfield
Architects

LONDON OLYMPIC STADIUM
Populous

LYRIC THEATRE, BELFAST
O'Donnell + Tuomey

MAGGIE'S GARTNAVEL, GLASGOW
OMA

NEW COURT, LONDON
OMA
with Allies & Morrison

The RIBA Stirling Prize, now in its seventeenth year is awarded to the architects of the building thought to be the most significant for the evolution of architecture and the built environment. A building is eligible for the prize if it is in the United Kingdom or is elsewhere in the European Union and is designed by a practice with an office in the UK. The shortlist is selected from RIBA Award-winners, and the winner receives £20,000 and a trophy designed by Morag Myerscough. The prize is named after the architect Sir James Stirling (1926–1992), one of the most important architects of his generation and a progressive thinker and designer throughout his career. The national media partner for the prize is The Observer; the Architects' Journal is the trade media partner.

The key criterion for any award given by the RIBA is that the project should demonstrate excellence. RIBA Awards juries assess design excellence irrespective of style, size or complexity of the project. They take into account constraints of budget, brief and timetable, and are sensitive to the economic and social contexts of each project.

Juries are asked in particular to judge the quality of the design of the scheme, particularly in respect of: the budget; the spatial experience that the scheme offers; the complexity of brief and degree of difficulty – the scheme's architectural ambition and ideas; its design vision; the selection and detailing of materials; the extent of innovation, invention and originality; the contract type; the appropriateness of the scheme's structural and servicing systems; fitness for purpose and the level of client satisfaction; the scheme's response to the issues of accessibility and sustainability and other social factors; its capacity to stimulate, engage and delight its occupants and visitors. Juries are required to judge what they see, not what they, as architects, might have done with a similar brief. They also understand that almost all buildings, even great works of architecture, have some flaws. An award-winning project should be capable of enduring as a fine work of architecture throughout its working life.

For previous winners of the prize, see page 214.

THE JUDGES

SIR NICHOLAS GRIMSHAW
CBE, PRA, AIA
Chairman Grimshaw Architects,
Chair of the RIBA Stirling Prize Jury
Sir Nicholas Grimshaw graduated from the Architectural Association in 1965. He immediately started his own practice and won many architectural awards for his buildings in the 1960s and 1970s. Sir Nicholas was elected Royal Academician in 1994 and was RA President between 2004 and 2011. In 1994 he was elected Honorary Fellow of the AIA. He was knighted by Her Majesty Queen Elizabeth II in 2002.

HILDE DAEM
Hilde Daem co-founded Robbrecht en Daem architecten in Ghent, Belgium in 1975. The practice often collaborates with artists in public spaces and they teamed up with Spanish artist Cristina Iglesias to design a project in front of the Royal Museum of Fine Arts, Antwerp. They are best known in the UK for their RIBA Award-winning Whitechapel Gallery (2010). In the same year she was made an RIBA International Fellow.

JOANNA VAN HEYNINGEN
MA (OXON), MA DIP ARCH (CANTAB)
Joanna van Heyningen set up her practice in 1977 and was joined in 1982 by Birkin Haward. She became a consultant to the practice in 2012. The practice's work is typified by the thoughtful organisation of plan and section in building and place-making. Weight, light and sound are constant themes, as is the importance of context. Joanna has taught and lectured widely and has been a member of the RIBA Awards Group.

NAOMI CLEAVER
While Naomi Cleaver is best known as presenter of Channel 4's *Grand Designs: Trade Secrets* she is primarily an interior, furniture and product designer whose work is characterised by a profound respect for architecture and a spirited sense of narrative. She worked for the design firm, Fitch, before establishing echo design, a 'dating agency' that matched new, exciting architecture and design practices, such as David Adjaye, with clients.

SIR MARK JONES, FRSE
Sir Mark Jones, art historian, numismatist and museum director, was director of the V&A from 2001 to 2011. He is the current Master of Saint Cross College, Oxford. Sir Mark's directorship of the National Museums of Scotland (1992-2001) saw the opening of the award-winning Museum of Scotland , the creation of the National War Museum of Scotland and the Museum of Scottish Country Life at Kittochside. He was knighted in 2010 for services to the arts.

Sainsbury Laboratory
Bateman Street, Cambridge

STANTON WILLIAMS

CLIENT: UNIVERSITY OF CAMBRIDGE
STRUCTURAL ENGINEER: AKT II
SERVICES ENGINEER: ARUP
LANDSCAPE: CHRISTOPHER BRADLEY-HOLE AND
SCHOENAICH LANDSCAPE ARCHITECTS
CONTRACTOR: KIER REGIONAL
CONTRACT VALUE: £69 MILLION
DATE OF COMPLETION: JANUARY 2011
GROSS INTERNAL AREA: 11,000 SQ M
IMAGES: HUFTON + CROW

The judges chose the Sainsbury Laboratory as the winner of
the 2012 RIBA Stirling Prize because they were impressed
by the building's calm beauty. This is a timeless piece
of architecture, sitting within a highly sensitive site, one
overlooking the woods where Darwin walked with his tutor
and mentor Henslow, discussing the origin of species. In this
project, Stanton Williams and their landscape architects have
created a new landscape, a courtyard which flows out into the
botanical gardens. The project is both highly particular and
specialised, and, at the same time, a universal building type,
taken to an extraordinary degree of sophistication and beauty.

The brief not only called for a building that facilitated
'world-class science', but also that it should achieve 'world-
class architecture'. According to client David Sainsbury,
'Scientists have traditionally been prepared to put up with
the most appalling conditions providing they are left alone to
get on with their work'. This project celebrates the laboratory,
an unloved type where boffins are thought never to look up
from their experiments or talk to one another. It has given

these scientists beautiful labs, all arranged on a single floor in an L-shape, with lovely views and gorgeous top light, which produces an extraordinary quality of shadowless light on the working surfaces. Despite the high energy demands of laboratories, the building has achieved a BREEAM Excellent rating, aided by 1,000 square metres of photovoltaic panels on the roof. A utilitarian building type has been elevated into the highest quality architecture, which communicates science as something glamorous and important.

The front of the building addresses the city of Cambridge, represented by a row of three-storey terraced houses. To avoid overlooking (in either direction), a colonnade of creamy stone shades the scientists' offices and allows windows to be opened. The façade's architectural austerity announces that this is a place where serious work goes on. Inside the entrance the floor gently ramps down towards a crossroads in the street. Turn right for the auditorium; turn left for the meeting rooms; take the broad shallow stair down to the Herbarium; take stairs or a ramp up to the laboratories. Here write-up areas form the ends of two promenades, flanked by small spontaneous brainstorming spaces with niche seating for sharing ideas and knowledge, and white boards for capturing inspiration. In between is the building's raison d'être, its heart: the laboratories, possibly the best in the world.

The project seems simple, and this hides the fact that it was a hugely difficult building to achieve. It needs to provide flexibility for future changes in scientific practice, and it achieves this brilliantly. The building balances openness with stringent requirements for security, which is achieved by placing the laboratories on the first floor. On the ground floor the public has invited access to the lecture theatre and meeting rooms. Here, too, is the charming café, fully open to the public, which sits between the gardens and the Sainsbury Laboratory's private courtyard, and from which one can watch the goings-on within. This forms the buffer between the private and public zones. Here visitors, as well as enjoying a coffee, can learn about the importance of the work that goes on in the laboratories and its contribution to the survival of our species.

The building uses fine materials expertly detailed; the judges loved the beautifully integrated works of art commissioned from Susanna Herron, William Pye and Norman Ackroyd. They were also impressed by the project's profound sustainability, not only in terms of its excellent energy performance, but also in terms of its long-term flexibility and adaptability. And they truly appreciated its classic timelessness.

The Hepworth Wakefield
Gallery Walk, Wakefield

DAVID CHIPPERFIELD ARCHITECTS

CLIENT: WAKEFIELD COUNCIL
STRUCTURAL ENGINEER: RAMBOLL UK
SERVICES ENGINEER: RAMBOLL UK
CONTRACTOR: LAING O'ROURKE NORTHERN
CONTRACT VALUE: £22.8 MILLION
DATE OF COMPLETION: MAY 2011
GROSS INTERNAL AREA: 5,232 SQ M
IMAGES: HUFTON + CROW

The promise of the building draws the visitor across an elegant entrance bridge, surrounded by all manner of strange river craft and motley post-industrial buildings. The gallery works beautifully with this varied and gritty context, both suggesting it belongs and at the same time is something rather special. Its scale shifts as you approach it; the carefully cast dusky mauve-grey concrete external forms make you want to stroke them.

This is a building for all seasons, which is important given its watery context: a horseshoe bend in the River Calder, the basin, the weir, the wharves, the bridge. And everywhere the urgent flow of the water. The northern elevations rise sheer out of the waters, like a castle from a moat. It took a major piece of engineering just to get it built: the river had to be dammed and the basin drained for six months while the foundations were dug. Constructed from pigmented in-situ concrete, the building is a conglomeration of differently sized trapezoidal blocks, each of different dimensions, grouped along the water's edge.

The programme is split horizontally between the ground floor and the first floor – which is exclusively used for exhibition space. The ground floor houses the shop, cafe, education room and offices, radiating out from the entrance space. The stair takes you up, wrapped in a beautiful, tactile grey MDF lining, to the first floor galleries. Here circulation takes the form of a promenade leading you through an enfilade of galleries. Now the external morphology can be understood: each volume represents and coincides with a single gallery, ceilings slope to match the outer roofs, no room is a parallelogram, giving each a unique atmosphere.

The galleries are formed using a double wall system which allows tolerance in the way the different gallery shapes relate to one other, providing wonderfully deep and substantial thresholds between spaces and completely concealing the ventilation services which feed in through floor level shadow gaps. Blackout is seamlessly integrated, as is daylight attenuation. The long slit rooflight is a recurring theme that models each space, while the carefully placed windows serve to rest the eye and constantly locate the building against the context of Hemsley Moor, the Town Hall, the weir and the Chapel on the Bridge.

For all the dramatic changes of scale, the spaces are focussed, comfortable and relaxed, allowing both large and small objects to be shown together in an atmosphere of intimacy. The fact that you can see from one space to another and sometimes beyond draws the eye naturally through, taking you with it. Open doorways link the gallery spaces in a fluid and varied sequence, offering tempting glimpses of other artworks and the outside world. The doughnut plan of overlapping rhomboids helps too.

The major galleries house permanent displays of large-scale sculptures and plaster casts by Barbara Hepworth and others, to highly light-sensitive works on paper from the City of Wakefield's collection of British art. The remaining rooms host a changing programme of temporary exhibitions. All of the galleries use the same neutral language, allowing for future reinterpretation and representation of art works. A system of flexible partitions allows for black box spaces to be created for video installations, without impairing the routes.

Visiting Hepworth is a truly uplifting experience and numbers have far exceeded expectations – many make a joint visit with the nearby Yorkshire Sculpture Park. The gallery is very focussed and perfectly considered. It gives the sense of being made specifically for the work of Hepworth whilst at the same time being very much of Yorkshire, grounded and granite-like. This is a life-affirming project on every level.

London Olympic Stadium
Queen Elizabeth Park, London E20

POPULOUS

CLIENT: OLYMPIC DELIVERY AUTHORITY
STRUCTURAL ENGINEER: BURO HAPPOLD
SERVICES ENGINEER: BURO HAPPOLD
ACOUSTICS CONSULTANTS: VANGUARDIA
LANDSCAPE ARCHITECT: HYLAND EDGAR
QUALITY SURVEYOR: ARCADIS AND CLM
CONTRACTOR: SIR ROBERT MCALPINE
CONTRACT VALUE: CONFIDENTIAL
DATE OF COMPLETION: MARCH 2012
GROSS INTERNAL AREA: 46,830 SQ M
IMAGES: LOCOG (BOTTOM; P. 27 TOP RIGHT); MORLEY VON STERNBERG
(P. 27 TOP LEFT; P. 28; P. 29); POPULOUS (TOP; P. 27 BOTTOM)

The hosting of the 2012 Olympic Games condensed 30 years of urban regeneration into just a decade, producing a series of new facilities in the largest new park to be built in London for over a hundred years. Central to the vision for 2012 was the creation not only of world-class venues for the period of the Games, but ones which also formed a legacy of sustainable facilities for future use by the people of London.

The design of the new Stadium, which formed the centre-piece of the Olympic and Paralympic Games, embraces this ambition, creating a world class venue seating 80,000 spectators for the main track and field events and ceremonies, which is capable of being transformed into a smaller scale venue accommodating 25,000. The design clearly expresses the main elements of the stadium, distinguishing between the white main structural elements (the horizontal members are lengths of left-over Russian gas pipe), the black secondary structures and the precast concrete of the seating tiers and plinth. The result is a striking and legible ensemble.

The structure is designed so it can be dismantled to form the smaller legacy venue, with the remaining elements capable of being recycled. The demountable nature of the structure is expressed through the simple and elegant detailing of its many connections and components.

The organisation focuses very much on the ease of movement for the large numbers of people who used the stadium during the Games. Spectators approached via a bridge across the canalised river that all but makes an island of the site. The water forms a natural barrier and means security on the 'island' could be less rigorous. The stadium wrap is made up of narrow sails of PVC that give wind protection at the upper levels and are twisted towards the ground to expose the gradated colours of the London Olympics, and to allow access from the arrival plinth. This runs round the full perimeter of the stadium, giving level wheelchair access. Because the bowl is cut into the ground, the entry point is half way up, making access easier for all, with half the spectators climbing to their seats, the other half descending. Movement is also simplified because the concourse is free of food outlets, which are instead accommodated in temporary pods outside the stadium. User satisfaction measured during the Olympics and Paralympics recorded that more than 97% were pleased with the facilities.

The bowl of the stadium provides for clear sightlines throughout and a surprisingly intimate relationship with the events for a venue of this scale. The architects and the client representatives fought hard to maintain this intimacy, arguing successfully that the athletes wanted to 'feel the breath of the spectators on them', so as to enhance their performances. The other crucial factor in a stadium is wind, so the partial roof is designed less to shelter (half) the spectators than to reduce eddies on the field: a tail wind of more than 2 metres per second means a record will not stand – such a head wind would mean they would not break records anyway. Usain Bolt set an Olympic record with a tail wind of 1.5 mps.

Back-of-house is simple, functional and egalitarian with the same palette used for royalty, sponsors and spectators. The design adeptly deals with an extremely demanding brief, creating on one hand a 'temporary' venue that engages with the sustainable agenda and legacy requirements, whilst also managing to create a landmark for the Games which, with its expressive and identifiable crown of rooftop floodlights on their triangular gantries, has become a landmark on the skyline of the city – one which it is hoped will survive in legacy mode.

Lyric Theatre
Belfast

O'DONNELL + TUOMEY

CLIENT: LYRIC THEATRE
STRUCTURAL ENGINEER: HORGAN LYNCH
SERVICES ENGINEER: IN2 ENGINEERING
CONTRACTOR: GLIBERT ASH
CONTRACT VALUE: £18 MILLION
DATE OF COMPLETION: MAY 2011
GROSS INTERNAL AREA: 5,026 SQ M
IMAGES: DENNIS GILBERT/VIEW

The new Lyric Theatre is a striking new home for a theatre with a unique status in Belfast – the only one with its own company. The architects responded to the considerable design challenges of its location with gusto. The steeply sloping river frontage within a tightly knit fabric of brick terraced houses presented a demanding agenda for a building type that requires large volumes to accommodate the auditorium, studio and rehearsal room. The Lyric Theatre meets that challenge admirably; the line of brick terraces seems to flow in to the Lyric's façade in a gentle crescendo. The theatre is at once self-effacing and self-confident, deferential and assertive.

The lobby accommodates a box office that does its modest job: that of selling 389 tickets for the main house, up to 170 for the studio theatre. Otherwise this is not a place to hang around, the theatre-goer is keen to mount the dramatic stair that snakes steeply up into the far richer spaces above

it. At the top of the first flight the space fans out into areas for gathering, for drinking, eating, for anticipating what is to come. The concrete is gorgeous, the joinery immaculate: the tactility of this area leads to the enveloping, dark and dramatic space of the main theatre itself. The architects share with Hertzberger a belief that the theatre is a place for people-watching as much as play-watching, and that extends beyond the gathering spaces into the auditorium itself, where the seats are angled in towards one another, cosying up, reinforcing the idea of theatre as a shared communal activity. This is a democratic space with a single shallow rake: no-one is more than sixteen rows back from the stage. The facetted walnut is rich aesthetically as well as acoustically. Its origami-like folds absorb and reflect back the actors' words in exact measures: the actors give this space great write-ups. The cladding was put together to tolerances of within one millimetre and John Tuomey says he has never before done anything as complicated as an auditorium.

If in the main space everything is prescribed, in the studio there is a blank canvas. This is a black box, except it isn't: with its brick walls, moderated by black drapes, it has the feel of a found space, a warehouse. Actors like that too, it makes them work harder.

The theatre is a factory for making plays in and its workforce – actors, stage-hands, wardrobe staff, front-of-house – deserve decent working conditions. Seldom is back-of-house as well done as it is here. Theatres are normally designed for audiences not actors, but here the route from the well-appointed, restful Green Room along corridors made of exactly the same materials as the public routes, lined with photographs of past productions, shows the hard-working actors the respect they deserve but so seldom receive. And although there is also a staff restroom-cum-café, with splendid terrace, the actors are just as often found mixing it with their audiences in the bar and restaurant. And it pays off, as director Conall Morrison says, 'all this loveliness ends up on stage.'

Belfast now has what is in all but name the National Theatre of Northern Ireland. The Lyric is a tangible portion of the peace dividend, which is why it was chosen as the meeting point for the Queen and Northern Ireland's Deputy First Minister Martin McGuinness to shake hands. The quality of the interior spaces, its sensitive response to a challenging site and the expansion of the Lyric's ability to function behind the scenes make this a stunning accomplishment and a pleasure to spend time in.

Maggie's Gartnavel
Glasgow

OMA

CLIENT: MAGGIE KESWICK JENCKS CANCER CARING CENTRES TRUST
STRUCTURAL ENGINEER: SINCLAIR KNIGHT MERZ
SERVICES ENGINEER: KJ TAIT ENGINEERS
LANDSCAPE: LILY JENCKS WITH HARRISON STEVENS
CONTRACTOR: DUNNE
CONTRACT VALUE: CONFIDENTIAL
DATE OF COMPLETION: 2011
IMAGES: PHILIPPE RUAULT

Glasgow's new Maggie's Centre, like its sister projects, sets out to provide space where people can feel welcome, at home and cared for – a haven. Set amid the austere, institutional and soulless hospital buildings, this seems like a tall order.

The architect has sited the building on a slight rise, but cleverly cut it into the slope so that on two sides it looks at banked landscape. It is mostly surrounded by dense tree planting, like a large cabin in pine woods. It is hard to imagine that just a short time ago this glade was a car park. The romantic backdrop is further enhanced by the abandoned Gothic bricked-up shell of a mental hospital.

Designed as a single storey, the Maggie's Centre strikes the visitor with its predominance of glazed walls in a doughnut plan. The entrance space reveals that the circuit is fully glazed on both elevations: looking out to the hospital surroundings with the internal elevation overlooking the landscape of the central courtyard. Simultaneously

one is aware of a series of interlocking rectangular spaces that lead away in a jagged, gently ramped circuit. In fact this overlapping of spaces feels surprisingly calm perhaps because of the flat ceiling plane, whereas the floor undulates around the ring via a series of short ramps that appear to follow the slope of the land. The consistent use of L-shaped solid 'wall' elements, (most containing cupboards, displays, desking, cloakrooms), gives a sense of place and security; vertical glazing completing the figural space opens the world internally and externally; and the processional interconnection creates an informal, almost carefree sense of permeability and promenade, most-tellingly avoiding that bane of hospital architecture – the corridor.

Much of Rem Koolhaas's work can be seen as a lifelong battle against the corridor. His best buildings are a series of spaces around which the building happens. But here counselling requires privacy every bit as much as does treatment (which only happens in the behemoth of the cancer hospital next door), so doors are a necessity. They slide shut to enclose discrete counselling rooms or private nooks and corners, or open to claim circulation space as their own. At least two of these places have involved local artist/artisan design and fabrication: a stack-layered undulating timber-lined room for quiet contemplation; and a full-height

backlit glass display wall, overlooking the set piece of every Maggie's: the kitchen table. There are no timetables here and no agendas. The centre's users just turn up to be welcomed with a cup of tea – and encouraged to relax, or exhale, the moment they walk through the sliding door.

There is a surprisingly rich variety of materials and skills on display here, with a particularly pleasing flush inlaid timber/concrete ceiling. Like the architects and all the consultants, the contractor gave his time for free, yet he was more than willing to experiment with the ceiling until it worked to perfection. The building is curiously introvert and extrovert at the same time. Nearly all the spaces relate to the landscape, which was designed by Maggie's daughter; either to the grassy banks, tree trunks and foliage outside or to the interior grassed mound, through floor-to-ceiling glass. The plan looks haphazard, even chaotic and there is a medley of different spaces and materials, but this is a masterful composition of highly-efficient spaces. Despite its seeming contradictions: introspective / extrovert, transparent / private, personal / communal, active / calm, it manages a connectedness, transparency and informal charm that meets the brief admirably to provide an uplifting refuge for those dealing with cancer, be they sufferers or their family and friends.

New Court
St Swithin's Lane London EC4

OMA WITH ALLIES & MORRISON

CLIENT: ROTHSCHILD
STRUCTURAL ENGINEER: ARUP
SERVICES ENGINEER: ARUP
COST CONSULTANT: DAVIS LANGDON
FIT-OUT ARCHITECT: PRINGLE BRANDON
LANDSCAPE: CHARLES FUNKE ASSOCIATES/INSIDE OUTSIDE
CONTRACTOR: LEND LEASE
CONTRACT VALUE: CONFIDENTIAL
DATE OF COMPLETION: OCTOBER 2011
GROSS INTERNAL AREA: 19,125 SQ M
IMAGES: CHARLIE KOOLHAAS (P. 39); OMA (TOP);
PHILIPPE RUAULT (BOTTOM; P. 40; P. 41)

Rothschild Bank has occupied the New Court site on London's St Swithin's Lane since 1809. This new corporate headquarters, the fourth iteration of Rothschild's London home, not only consolidates the Bank's previously dispersed facilities within one building but also makes a number of important urban moves, reinstating the historic visual connection between St Swithin's and Christopher Wren's neighbouring Church of St Stephen Walbrook, hidden from public view by previous New Court developments.

OMA and Allies & Morrison worked closely with City Planner Peter Rees and his team for 18 months, adjusting the design in order to achieve planning consent for a building twice the height of any of its neighbours, including Mansion House and the Bank of England.

The new building is organised into a central cube capped with a smaller rooftop tower, surrounded by three adjoining annexes which contain the main circulation and allow uninterrupted office floors within the central cube, with abundant daylight and views out to the City beyond. The central cube is lifted above St Swithin's Lane by a series of pilotis that create a wider cloistered edge and a raised covered entrance square. This sequence of new public realm and vistas both gives something back to improve the quality of the everyday life and streetscape of the City and lends a quiet public presence to this previously private institution.

The attention to detail and the combination of materials both give a sense of underlying, understated elegance, heightened by the considered contrast of original paintings and artefacts beautifully displayed and lit in vitrines, and the quirky use of super-scale graphics and photo blow-ups. OMA's interest in fabrics and print is evident everywhere on the upper floors, where rooms for meetings, dining and functions are decorated with a mix of images screen printed, woven into tapestries or etched on to metal. The images are all drawn from Rothschild's collection of fine and decorative arts and archives. The latter are stored on-site in a delightful book-lined room with oak joinery by the Mouseman of Kilburn, North Yorkshire: Robert Thompson whose mark is the carved mouse on every piece to leave the workshop. This archive opens directly on to the entrance square and its intimacy contrasts with the generosity of the volume that houses the lobby, whose lively acoustic is somewhat softened by the full-length drapes by OMA.

The office floors in the principal cube are immaculately fitted out by Pringle Brandon – every decision about furnishings, fittings and finishes is just so. The floors are linked by an internal wooden stair which facilitates communication and exercise (though this is also taken care of by a decent-sized gym – staff are well looked after too, with a well-made staff canteen which more resembles an upmarket restaurant, while more senior staff have access to the use of the family silver and a private dining room). Best of all is the amount of daylight the office floors benefit from. Although the open-plan floors have a perimeter of cellular offices, these glass boxes scarcely disrupt the daylight at all. What also helps is the generous ceiling heights. The whole scheme was delivered by Allies & Morrison whose professional expertise ensured that the client got exactly what they needed.

The building culminates in the fourth annexe, a 'sky pavilion' lifted above the office cube to create a rooftop loggia and garden. It contains a series of meeting, dining and function rooms within two double-height volumes offering panoramic views across the City and the Thames. A hydraulic lift with a housing of glass as its only expression in the main function room links the two floors. The City has a new and surprising masterpiece.

THE RIBA
LUBETKIN PRIZE

THE WINNER

**GUANGZHOU INTERNATIONAL
FINANCE CENTRE**
GUANGZHOU, CHINA
Wilkinson Eyre Architects

THE SHORTLIST

ONE KL
KUALA LUMPUR, MALAYSIA
SCDA Architects

SOLARIS @ ONE-NORTH
SINGAPORE
TR Hamzah and Yeang
in collaboration with
CPG Consultants

SPERONE WESTWATER
NEW YORK, USA
Foster + Partners

The RIBA Lubetkin Prize is awarded to the architect of the best RIBA International Award-winning building. Buildings eligible for RIBA International Awards are those outside the European Union designed by RIBA Chartered Architects or RIBA International Fellows.

The prize is named after Berthold Lubetkin (1901–1990), the architect from Georgia who emigrated to Britain in the 1930s and went on to establish the radical architecture group Tecton. He is best known for the two Highpoint buildings in Highgate, London (1933–38), and for the Penguin Pool at London Zoo (1934). The pool provided the inspiration for the plaque designed and made by the artist Petr Weigl. The plaque was presented to the winner of the Lubetkin Prize at the RIBA Stirling Prize Dinner.

For previous winners of the prize, see page 214.

THE VISITING JUDGES

DEBORAH SAUNT
Architect, DSDHA
Chair of RIBA Awards Group

TONY CHAPMAN
RIBA Head of Awards

THE FULL JURY

Visiting judges plus:

ANGELA BRADY
RIBA President

CINDY WALTERS
Architect Walters & Cohen

PHILIP GUMUCHDJIAN
Gumuchdjian Architects

Guangzhou International Finance Centre
Guangzhou, China

WILKINSON EYRE ARCHITECTS

CLIENT: GUANGZHOU YUEXIU CITY CONSTRUCTION
STRUCTURAL ENGINEER: ARUP
SERVICES ENGINEER: ARUP
CONTRACTOR: CHINA STATE CONSTRUCTION CORPORATION
CONTRACT VALUE: £600 MILLION
DATE OF COMPLETION: JUNE 2011
GROSS INTERNAL AREA: 380,000 SQ M
IMAGES: JONATHAN LEIJONHUFVUD (P. 43; BOTTOM; OPPOSITE; P. 47 TOP);
CHRISTIAN RICHTERS (TOP; P. 46 TOP); WEA (P. 46 BOTTOM; P. 47 BOTTOM)

The Guangzhou International Finance Centre proves that wherever it goes, British architecture can make a difference. Wilkinson Eyre won the competition with a slender, plectrum-shaped mixed-use tower rising to 103 storeys out of a podium containing shopping and a connection to the subway system and three levels of parking, as well as two linked smaller towers of accommodation.

The main tower is 66 floors of offices and 38 floors of a Four Seasons hotel arranged around a dramatic tapering atrium. For all the smoothness of its crystalline skin, this is a building that expresses its diagrid structure to the world through its glazed façades and internally to the user of every office and hotel room through the presence of the raked concrete-filled steel tubes that form the structure.

The beauty of the diagrid is in its inherent stiffness, which in turn gives it its strength. It also means the tower needs no 'damping', yet is still a comfortable building in which to work. Each diamond is 54 metres or twelve storeys high, reducing the amount of steel required for the construction by a remarkable 20%. What is more, the ratio of floor plan to envelope makes this a highly efficient building.

Originally it was designed with a double skin, a plan that fell victim to the client's understandable desire for more floor space. Instead the sun protection that a double skin would have afforded has had to be built into the glass – hence the dark grey appearance, a distinctive merit of the finished tower.

This is a hugely complex project that appears to be extraordinarily simple, like most of the best things in life. In a culture where showing off is generally required by clients of their architects, the IFF is refreshingly elegant and easy on the eye.

The judges made the Guangzhou International Finance Centre the winner of the 2012 RIBA Lubetkin Prize because it is a building that is truly iconic, an object of wonder on the city skyline. The architects have gone way beyond the demands of commercial clients to produce a piece of world architecture that contributes to the public realm through its sheer beauty.

One KL
Kuala Lumpur, Malaysia

SCDA ARCHITECTS

CLIENT: WATERFRONT GROUP
STRUCTURAL ENGINEER: SHIMIZU CORPORATION
SERVICES ENGINEER: SHIMIZU CORPORATION
CONTRACTOR: SHIMIZU CORPORATION
CONTRACT VALUE: CONFIDENTIAL
DATE OF COMPLETION: MARCH 2010
GROSS INTERNAL AREA: 45,245 SQ M
IMAGES: AARON POCOCK (TOP; P. 49; P. 50 BOTTOM; P. 51);
ALBERT LIM (BOTTOM; P. 50 TOP)

One KL is a 35 storey residential tower with a prestige to match the exclusivity of its address. Each duplex has its own pool, rectangular or L-shaped depending on the location of the apartment. These mini-infinity pools are expressed on the façade with glass end-walls, making them an outward manifestation of the desirability of the accommodation within. As a result these places sell themselves.

The tower is C shaped so as to make the best use of a tight urban site. It means that it has three fronts and three backs, the missing fourth elevation draws the wind, negative pressure pushing it up the void and cross ventilating the structure through the cuts made by the terraces and pools. Condensation produced by the air crossing the pools also results in local cooling.

The dual aspect of each apartment has other advantages. It brings light into all the rooms, not least the inevitable servants' quarters, transforming their living and working conditions. It also produces what is probably architecturally the most interesting space – the void with its dramatic escape stairs. Another space which benefits from the indoor-outdoor ambiguity is the third-level slice of communal living comprising pool, gardens, gym and multi-functional space.

On the outside the architects have played with the grid, alternately sliding the apartments to the left or the right to allow for the pools and terraces, so that the units interlink, giving these elevations a rhythm that enlivens the whole composition. Internally the generosity of the spaces allows the interest to be continued with double and single-height spaces interlocking, so that a mezzanine corridor overlooking the living-dining spaces, joins the bedrooms. In the penthouses the device continues on up through a further two floors to a magnificent roof terrace.

Kuala Lumpur has some of the highest levels of humidity in the world – 95% being common. This building, by architects who have been working on the problem for more than a decade, has apartments that go far beyond the anodyne air-conditioned boxes that even the richest seem to be generally content with.

Solaris
Fusionopolis 2B, One North, Singapore

TR HAMZAH AND YEANG
IN COLLABORATION WITH CPG CONSULTANTS
CLIENT: SOILBUILD GROUP HOLDINGS
STRUCTURAL ENGINEER: ARUP SINGAPORE
SERVICES ENGINEER: CPG CONSULTANTS
CONTRACTOR: SOIL-BUILD
CONTRACT VALUE: £49.9 MILLION
DATE OF COMPLETION: MARCH 2011
GROSS INTERNAL AREA: 51,274 SQ M
IMAGES: ALBERT LIM; FOO E-JIN (P. 54 TOP)

Ken Yeang's approach to designing buildings to cope naturally with extreme climates has been hugely important and his ideas disseminated in a series of influential books. But it is only when you see one of his buildings that you understand that they work aesthetically as well as they do environmentally.

Solaris is two big buildings, one seven, one fourteen storeys, linked by a generous daylit and naturally ventilated atrium with rooflights that close automatically when it rains and crossed by sky-bridges at high level. A rain-check glass wall made up of glazing separated by perforated panels also keeps out the rain while allowing cross ventilation.

This is a green building in every sense of the word. A narrow landscaped ramp, more like a stony country path, wraps itself round the building for 1.5 kilometres, rising from

ground level up to a roof garden with dramatic views of one third of Singapore. It provides walks for the buildings' users and a habitat for birds, butterflies and even the occasional snake. Altogether the landscaping exceeds the amount of greenfield land taken up by the building by 13% – giving it an impressive Green Mark rating of 113%. Included within this figure are the sky terraces, where the linear path broadens out into wide hard landscaped but well-planted terraces where staff can meet up – an important provision in a building whose primary function is scientific research and development.

Precisely shaped sun-shading louvres supplement the hard-working low-emissivity glass, resulting in relatively cool open plan office spaces even when the air con is turned off. In the deeper plan of the two buildings, a broad light-well or 'solar shaft' runs diagonally through the section, scooping light into the heart of the building and reducing the need for artificial lighting. Rainwater harvesting stores enough water (700 cubic metres) underground to irrigate the landscaping for five days.

Consq!uently Solaris has very low carbon emissions, just 62 kilograms of carbon per square metre. The result is a building that has achieved the local Building and Construction Authority's Green Mark Platinum Standard. This is a building where the organic meets the inorganic in a most satisfying and pleasing manner.

Sperone Westwater
Bowery, New York City, USA

FOSTER + PARTNERS

CLIENT: SPERONE WESTWATER
STRUCTURAL ENGINEER: BURO HAPPOLD
SERVICES ENGINEER: BURO HAPPOLD
CONTRACTOR: SCIAME
CONTRACT VALUE: CONFIDENTIAL
DATE OF COMPLETION: SEPTEMBER 2010
GROSS INTERNAL AREA: 1,858 SQ M
IMAGES: NIGEL YOUNG FOSTER + PARTNERS

A sensitive, sympathetic client, a generous budget, a programme built on selling the art of some of the world's top artists in one of New York's longest established private galleries – it sounds like a dream commission. And then there is the site: just 7.6 metres wide by 30.5 metres deep, a narrow slot in the Bowery, amid the second-hand kitchenware stores. In less able hands this site could have produced a curator's nightmare. Instead this is a mature, thoughtful and polished piece of work: a curator's dream.

Externally, by day this building is as tough as any in the Bowery, a slender milled glass fortress that relates in scale to the building around it. By day it has the air of fine steel, by night its transparency shines through, not least in the moving room. This additional 6 by 3 metre gallery space is also the goods lift which can be parked at any of the four floors of galleries above the entrance level. If it is in use as an extended gallery space, then circulation is via the lift and stair core towards the rear of the building. Only ground conditions prevented the moving room from descending to occupy the street level entry. This leads through to a double-height long gallery and a further, smaller one, intriguingly top-lit courtesy of a set-back to the floors above on the rear elevation. A smoothly curved mezzanine gallery overlooking the long gallery leads to a sculpture terrace above a secret garden 'borrowed' from the adjacent apartment block. The progression of galleries continues upwards, each floor subtly different in plan and feel: a conventional gallery topped with two 'his and her' floors reflecting the different styles of the two owners, Sperone and Westwater; then up again to offices (which could become another gallery) and finally a library and archive worthy of any grand villa.

This is a gallery which perfectly serves both its private and public functions: discreet rooms for conversations with potential buyers and public galleries as fine as any in New York City drawing an appreciative public. This is architecture that advertises its subject and itself equally well. A little masterpiece.

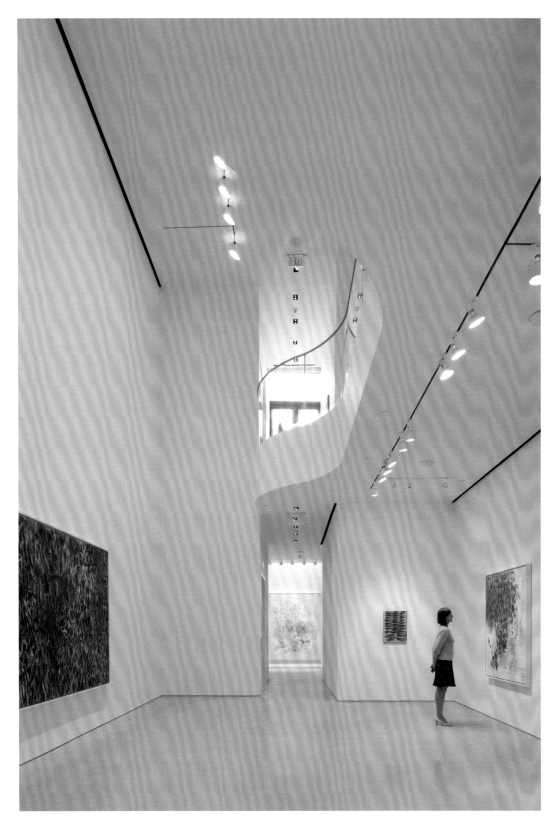

THE RIBA INTERNATIONAL *and* EUROPEAN AWARDS

Auckland Art Gallery
– Toi O Tāmaki
Auckland, New Zealand

FJMT + ARCHIMEDIA
– ARCHITECTS IN ASSOCIATION

CLIENT: AUCKLAND COUNCIL
STRUCTURAL ENGINEER: HOLMES CONSULTING GROUP
SERVICES ENGINEER: AECOM
CONTRACTOR: HAWKINS CONSTRUCTION
CONTRACT VALUE: £64 MILLION
DATE OF COMPLETION: OCTOBER 2011
GROSS INTERNAL AREA: 14,370 SQ M
IMAGES: JOHN GOLLINGS; PATRICK REYNOLDS (MIDDLE RIGHT)

The Auckland Art Gallery – Toi o Tāmaki – wanted to double its gallery space by restoring and adapting its historic galleries, dating from 1887, and creating a new exhibition area to complement them. A series of emblematic, sculpted tree-like canopies enclose the forecourt, atrium and gallery areas, inspired by a nearby grove of pohutukawa trees and creating a new organic identity to the gallery. The canopies are supported by slender, tapering shafts and the soffits are of geometrically cut timber from massive Kauri trees, traditionally used by the Maori peoples for house- and boatbuilding. The result is a delightful sequence of transparent, naturally-lit galleries in which internal and external views are created to provide rich backgrounds for the art and to enhance the experience of the gallery visitor.

Balsillie School of International Affairs, CIGI Campus
Canada

KUWABARA PAYNE MCKENNA BLUMBERG
ARCHITECTS
CLIENT: CENTRE FOR INTERNATIONAL GOVERNANCE INNOVATION
STRUCTURAL ENGINEER: BLACKWELL BOWICK PARTNERSHIP
SERVICES ENGINEER: CROSSEY ENGINEERING
CONTRACTOR: COOPER CONSTRUCTION
CONTRACT VALUE: £60 MILLION
DATE OF COMPLETION: SEPTEMBER 2011
GROSS INTERNAL AREA: 9,300 SQ M
IMAGES: MARIS MEZULIS (TOP; BOTTOM); TOM ARBAN (MIDDLE)

The clients wanted a sustainable building that would last a
century and would befit its site, the former historic Seagram
Distillery, bounded by three Governor General Award-
winning projects (Canada's highest architectural award). The
architects have responded to the client's wish for a 'vibrant
sanctuary', and a design that is 'functional but not fancy', with
a contemporary reinterpretation of a traditional Oxford quad
complete with courtyard and bell tower. They have gone for a
restful palette of limestone, brick, Douglas Fir and glass.
The plan organises two long three-storey interconnecting
buildings and an auditorium pavilion around a generous
landscaped courtyard. This is one of the first buildings in
Ontario to use Bubble Deck systems, in which recycled plastic
balls replace 30% of the non-structural concrete.

Clayton Campus
Monash University
Melbourne, Australia

BVN ARCHITECTURE

CLIENT: MONASH UNIVERSITY
STRUCTURAL ENGINEER: BONACCI GROUP
SERVICES ENGINEER: NORMAN DISNEY YOUNG
CONTRACTOR: BROAD APM
CONTRACT VALUE: £44 MILLION
DATE OF COMPLETION: DECEMBER 2011
GROSS INTERNAL AREA: 22,000 SQ M
IMAGES: JOHN GROLLINGS

This large student housing project comprises two 5-storey buildings each housing 300 students arranged with a 'boomerang' plan facing each other to form an elongated diamond-shaped courtyard. The plan produces a large sheltered communal space that has a delightful collegiate feel to it. The simple palette of timber, glass, concrete and black steel that makes up the whole exterior of the building produces a modest but pleasing result. There has been a significant investment in large solar PV and solar hot water arrays, water recycling and natural ventilation with thermal chimneys, resulting in a 5* Australian Green Star rating. This is a creditable and credible application of modern sustainable design principles on a significant scale in a relatively low cost design and build project.

Frick Chemistry Laboratory
Princeton University, United States

HOPKINS ARCHITECTS

CLIENT: PRINCETON OFFICE OF DESIGN AND CONSTRUCTION
STRUCTURAL ENGINEER: ARUP
SERVICES ENGINEER: ARUP
CONTRACTOR: TURNER CONSTRUCTION COMPANY
CONTRACT VALUE: CONFIDENTIAL
DATE OF COMPLETION: JANUARY 2011
GROSS INTERNAL AREA: 24,620 SQ M
IMAGES: WARREN JAGGER

Princeton University wanted a sustainable building to re-house its chemistry department. Hopkins response has been in their classic manner: the building is a subtle composition of a laboratory wing and three blocks of offices and staircase cores, all linked by a lofty atrium that extends the social space out towards the surrounding landscape, and gives a sense of transparency to the normally hermetic world of the laboratories. The lab benches extend to the perimeter, giving views to and from the outside and into the atrium. The environmental strategy sets new standards of environmental performance for laboratory buildings, employing chilled beams, photo-voltaics, and rainwater and grey water recycling. It is a building that should last well and be adaptable to future changing needs in laboratory design.

Innhouse
Kunming, China

INTEGER INTELLIGENT AND GREEN

CLIENT: HEXY HORTI-EXPO XING YUN REAL ESTATE
STRUCTURAL ENGINEER: HYDER CONSULTING
CONTRACTOR: HEXY HORTI-EXPO XING YUN REAL ESTATE
CONTRACT VALUE: CONFIDENTIAL
DATE OF COMPLETION: DECEMBER 2011
GROSS INTERNAL AREA: 4,350 SQ M
IMAGES: KERON IP

The architects have responded well to the idyllic mountain context, breaking up the luxury boutique hotel into a series of carefully sculpted pavilions. Slatted vertical cedar timber covers much of the outsides of the buildings, with the slats being spaced out where they are positioned over windows, providing screening from solar gain. The blocks and their cantilevered balconies are held up by a concealed steel-framing system, heightening the sense of openness and drama within the densely forested location. The project possesses good sustainability credentials for a luxury hotel. It uses locally sourced timber and other materials, and has low U-values and carefully placed opening windows to minimise heat gain and thus cut down on the air-conditioning load.

The Troika
Kuala Lumpur

FOSTER + PARTNERS

CLIENT: BANDAR RAYA DEVELOPMENTS
STRUCTURAL ENGINEER: WEB STRUCTURES
SERVICES ENGINEER: JURUTERA PERUNDING VALDUN
CONTRACTOR: IJM CORPORATION BERHAD
CONTRACT VALUE: CONFIDENTIAL
DATE OF COMPLETION: JUNE 2011
GROSS INTERNAL AREA: 75,000 SQ M
IMAGES: NIGEL YOUNG

This daring attempt to find a new functionally-driven form for high-density urban living in tropical climates combines apartments, offices, shops and restaurants in three unequal towers clustered around an enclosed courtyard. The twisting geometry of the towers responds organically to neighbouring buildings, solar orientation and distant views. The delight in non-orthogonal form is enhanced by the unusual structural system of intriguingly slender concrete walls supporting stacked blocks of apartments which shift subtly in plan and orientation to focus on the best available views and add to the sense of movement in the building. In a climate where shade and wind-driven ventilation provide the only natural means of tempering the excessive heat, the apartments are designed so that they can be naturally ventilated when the weather allows.

Urban housing and crèche
Geneva, Switzerland

SERGISON BATES ARCHITECTS
WITH JEAN-PAUL JACCAUD ARCHITECTES

CLIENT: FONDATION VILLE DE GENÈVE POUR LE LOGEMENT SOCIAL
STRUCTURAL ENGINEER: SANCHA
CONTRACTOR: SERGISON BATES WITH JEAN-PAUL JACCAUD ARCHITECTS
CONTRACT VALUE: £8.83 MILLION
DATE OF COMPLETION: SEPTEMBER 2011
GROSS INTERNAL AREA: 3,476 SQ M
IMAGES: DAVID GRANDORGE

The building is inserted into the existing urban structure of arcades, covered walkways, alleys and yards, with a variety of openings and routes that create a sense of permeability within a dense city block. A new arcade makes it possible to walk down the length of the street under cover. The entrance to the crèche has the familiar detail of a shopfront, and allows views into the rear courtyard, a shaded and secure play-space for the children. The apartments are organised around the perimeter of the site on all four sides, with central halls connecting rooms in a continuous spatial sequence. The new building stitches and weaves itself into the texture of the city, with a façade of rich and layered elements.

Yotsuya Tenera
Tokyo, Japan

KEY OPERATION INC / ARCHITECTS

CLIENT: PRIVATE
STRUCTURAL ENGINEER: DELTA STRUCTUAL CONSULTANTS
SERVICES ENGINEER: COMODO
CONTRACTOR: FUJIKI KONUTEN
CONTRACT VALUE: CONFIDENTIAL
DATE OF COMPLETION: DECEMBER 2011
GROSS INTERNAL AREA: 380 SQ M
IMAGES: TOSHIHIRO SOBAJIMA

Situated in a residential district of Tokyo, the three-storey Yotsuya Tenera building occupies a curved site and complies with a number of onerous planning constraints, such as having to build away from boundaries of the site, rights to light and evacuation requirements. While meeting these demands, the architects have succeeded in creating a building of coherence and complexity, with twelve distinct types of apartment accessed from two day-lit and naturally ventilated stairs that eliminate the need for any corridors. Conceived as voids within solid concrete masses, the generosity of these stairs belies their size, being tightly and efficiently planned without being at all claustrophobic. The communal stair encourages interaction between residents without compromising privacy and each unit has either a balcony or terrace.

Bilbao Arena and Sports Centre
Spain

IDOM

CLIENT: AZPIEGITURAK
STRUCTURAL ENGINEER: IDOM
SERVICES ENGINEER: IDOM
CONTRACTOR: UTE CYCASA OHL
CONTRACT VALUE: CONFIDENTIAL
DATE OF COMPLETION: SEPTEMBER 2010
GROSS INTERNAL AREA: 30,808 SQ M
IMAGES: JORGE ALLENDE

This 20,000 seat professional basketball stadium and
community sports centre is perched on the grassy outcrop of
a former Bilbao iron ore mine. The veil of green painted steel
'leaves' hangs five metres beyond the world-class basketball
arena inside. This creates an exterior service zone (like the
branches of a tree) for the building's gloriously accessible
array of air-handling equipment. In total contrast to the
light-footed dance of the basketball arena structure, the
community sports centre is a cave carved from the ferrous
rock. Low-level pool lighting and dark materials give this 'local
public amenity' space an aura of five star hotel glamour and
tranquility. Its combination of spatial and material creativity,
inventive detailing and strict discipline has produced an
exemplary new building at very low cost.

Centre Pompidou
Metz, France

SHIGERU BAN AND JEAN DE GASTINE ARCHITECTES
WITH GUMUCHDJIAN ARCHITECTS

CLIENT: CA2M AND CITY OF METZ
STRUCTURAL ENGINEER: OVE ARUP/TERRELL INTERNATIONAL
SERVICES ENGINEER: OVE ARUP
CONTRACTOR: DEMATHIEU & BARD
CONTRACT VALUE: £51 MILLION
DATE OF COMPLETION: MAY 2010
GROSS INTERNAL AREA: 17,600 SQ M
IMAGES: HUFTON + CROW

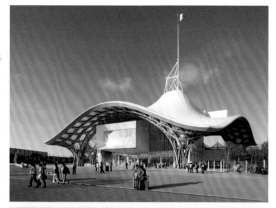

This was an ambitious project to provide a world class art gallery, to regenerate a run-down area in Metz. The result is a building like no other, its brilliant successes deriving from its precise conceptual response to the difficult brief, which called for three flexible rectangular galleries 90m by 15m. They are are expressed as exuded tubes, stacked above each other and pointing in different directions, with solid side walls and glazed end walls giving panoramic views to the outside. A vast naturally ventilated and unheated public space, enclosed by polycarbonate walls, for events and displays, is oversailed by a great woven timber roof canopy, likened by Shigeru Ban to a Chinese bamboo hat. It is a unique and extraordinary achievement.

FCN 2009 – House in Noto
Sicily

MARIA GIUSEPPINA GRASSO CANNIZZO

CLIENT: FEDERICA CIMATTI
STRUCTURAL ENGINEER: PRO GE CO/ICP
CONTRACTOR: ICP
CONTRACT VALUE: £180,000
DATE OF COMPLETION: APRIL 2011
GROSS INTERNAL AREA: 115 SQ M
IMAGES: HELENE BINET
MIDLISTED FOR THE RIBA STIRLING PRIZE

Situated on the side of a hill, at the end of a dirt track, in a seismic area, this house, built for €150,000, is a lesson in freshness of thinking, invention and in the inseparable nature of structure and architecture. An apparently solid plywood-clad box floats above the site, pitched so as to enjoy the horizon and the distant sea. It prizes open by means of a movable guest-wing, mechanically operated, which slides away to reveal a terrace and a glass wall to the main house. The main fixed element of the house is constructed in prefabricated concrete. A visit to this house provides a breath of fresh air, it displays imagination, playfulness, skill, invention and economy of means which is so often absent in contemporary work.

H27D
Konstanz, Germany

KRAUS SCHOENBERG ARCHITECTS

CLIENT: DOSER + PARTNER BAUGESELLSCHAFT MBH
STRUCTURAL ENGINEER: FISCHER & LEISERING
SERVICES ENGINEER: GREINER ENGINEERING
CONTRACTOR: KARL STOCKER BAUUNTERNEHMEN GMBH
CONTRACT VALUE: CONFIDENTIAL
DATE OF COMPLETION: APRIL 2011
GROSS INTERNAL AREA: 930 SQ M
IMAGES: IOANA MARINESCU

H27D represents an elegant combination of sensitivity to context and technical prowess. The walls are made entirely of lightweight concrete blocks, avoiding the use of additional thermal insulation or membranes. The fair-faced concrete is undressed both inside and out and would be easily demountable. The material is completely recyclable and achieves zero waste requirements. The apartments are deep in plan and ingenious. A typical plan has small bedrooms with a linking balcony overlooking the street, with a large open-plan L-shaped living-kitchen-dining area behind. This clever mixed use scheme of 930 square metres (a clothes shop occupies the whole of the ground floor giving it a real street presence) was achieved in a conservation area at the remarkable price of 1,428 euros per square metre.

Las Arenas
Barcelona, Spain

ROGERS STIRK HARBOUR + PARTNERS

CLIENT: METROVACESA
STRUCTURAL ENGINEER: EXPEDITION ENGINEERING
SERVICES ENGINEER: BOMA
CONTRACTOR: DRAGADOS
CONTRACT VALUE: CONFIDENTIAL
DATE OF COMPLETION: MARCH 2011
GROSS INTERNAL AREA: 105,816 SQ M
IMAGES: DAVID CARDELUS

This is a radical transformation of a redundant bull-fighting arena into an enormous leisure and entertainment complex. The removal of the mound on which the bull-ring sat and the excavation of five levels of basement car parking has involved some heroic engineering. The brick elevations are clasped by concrete beams, supported by raking legs and braced by a new steel structure which forms a running track around the building. Inside, concrete columns support radial cantilevered steel cinema pods. More characteristic yellow steel legs support a 100 metre diameter dish with a laminated timber gridshell roof. Skirting this structure is a cantilvered public 'plaza in the sky', with bars and restaurants enjoying wonderful panoramic views of Barcelona. A veritable *tour de force*.

PJ Carroll's Factory
Dundalk, Ireland

SCOTT TALLON WALKER ARCHITECTS

CLIENT: MR CONOR LAIT
STRUCTURAL ENGINEER: ARUP CONSULTING ENGINEERS
SERVICES ENGINEER: BDP BUILDING DESIGN PARTNERSHIP
CONTRACTOR: SISK
CONTRACT VALUE: £17.7 MILLION
DATE OF COMPLETION: SEPTEMBER 2010
GROSS INTERNAL AREA: 10,000 SQ. M
IMAGES: JOHN DONAT (TOP); PAUL TIERNEY; ROS KAVANAGH

It is not often a firm gets a chance do a makeover in terms of both form and function of one of their masterpieces. The major design decision taken was to organise the offices around three atria, two of which are organized as a restaurant and a wintergarden. All this required three 20 by 20 metre bays to be jacked up by a metre to create two-storey accommodation. This a project that has rescued an important example of mid-century modernism and given it new use and new life. It answers many of the questions raised by the global economic crisis about how best and most economically can we re-use under-performing and outmoded structures, rather than building from scratch.

Solid 11
Amsterdam

TONY FRETTON ARCHITECTS

CLIENT: STADGENOOT PROJECTONTWIKKELING
STRUCTURAL ENGINEER: DHV
CONTRACTOR: COEN HAGEDOORN BOUW
CONTRACT VALUE: £18.3 MILLION
DATE OF COMPLETION: JUNE 2011
GROSS INTERNAL AREA: 8,000 SQ M
IMAGES: PETER COOK
MIDLISTED FOR THE RIBA STIRLING PRIZE

The client sees his projects as 'providing a need, not a profit'; they are designed to last for a century and so have to be adaptable to the needs of unknown occupants. The spaces in this building were auctioned off on completion in one day, and the successful bidders (the chief architect was not one of them) were decided upon on the basis of their financial offer but also what they would bring to the mix of the building. Uses include cafes, restaurants, boutique hotels, a dentist, a hairdresser, and artists, alongside regular residential uses. What Tony Fretton has achieved is to deliver a building with endless possibilities by providing light, tough and in some places ingenious spaces.

Wexford County Council Headquarters
Wexford, Ireland

ROBIN LEE ARCHITECTURE IN ASSOCIATION WITH
ARTHUR GIBNEY AND PARTNERS

CLIENT: WEXFORD COUNTY COUNCIL
STRUCTURAL ENGINEER: BURO HAPPOLD
SERVICES ENGINEER: BURO HAPPOLD
CONTRACTOR: WEXFORD COUNTY COUNCIL
CONTRACT VALUE: £41 MILLION
DATE OF COMPLETION: JUNE 2011
GROSS INTERNAL AREA: 11,500 SQ M
IMAGES: ANDREW LEE
MIDLISTED FOR THE RIBA STIRLING PRIZE

Wexford County Council Headquarters will probably be the last and is arguably one of the most successful of the range of local government buildings built in Ireland over the last decade. An internal plaza that delights in shade and light unites the six departmental buildings housed in separate blocks separated by sheltered, lushly planted outdoor courtyards. Each has its own threshold space onto the shared plaza and its own central atrium that provides individual identity. A glazed skin wraps the whole building, providing shelter from the wind on a very exposed site so that windows opening into it admit tempered air. Together these strategies help to drive a natural ventilation scheme that is very carefully considered in what is ultimately a relatively deep plan building.

THE RIBA MANSER MEDAL

THE WINNER

MAISON L
YVELINES, FRANCE
Christian Pottgiesser,
architecturespossibles

THE SHORTLIST

THE DUNE HOUSE
SUFFOLK
Jarmund Vigsnæs Architects
and Mole Architects

PRIVATE HOUSE
GLOUCESTERSHIRE
Found Associates

PRIVATE HOUSE
EAST SUSSEX
Duggan Morris Architects

**TWO PASSIVE SOLAR GAIN
HOUSES**
CORNWALL
Simon Conder Associates

The RIBA Manser Medal is awarded to the best one-off new house or major extension designed by an architect in the European Union.

The objective of the RIBA Manser Medal has always been to encourage innovation in house design, to show how social and technological ambitions can be met by intelligent design and to produce exemplars to be taken up by the wider house-building industry. The prize is named after Michael Manser, former President of the RIBA, who is well known for his own steel and glass house designs.

Michael had for a number of years chaired the National Homebuilder Design Awards, which were run by Mike Gazzard HON FRIBA. He approached Tony Chapman, custodian of all the RIBA's awards then and now, about how to mark Michael Manser's contribution. It was agreed to create an award in his name for one-off houses – by way of balancing the Housing Design Awards which are exclusively for housing. It was presented as part of the National Homebuilder Design Awards for two years, before switching stables in 2003 to become part of the RIBA Awards. In 2006 the National Homebuilder Design Awards were bought by EMAP, long-term sponsors of the RIBA's awards programme. The award has since been presented at the RIBA Awards Dinner and latterly at the RIBA Stirling Prize Dinner, even twice being televised.

The award was judged by Michael Manser CBE, Stuart Piercy, Tony Chapman, Lady Ritblat and David Scott.

Maison L
Paris, France

ARCHITECTURESPOSSIBLES

CLIENT: PRIVATE
STRUCTURAL ENGINEER: JOEL BETITO
CONTRACTOR: LES CONSTRUCTEURS DE SURESNES
CONTRACT VALUE: CONFIDENTIAL
DATE OF COMPLETION: AUGUST 2011
GROSS INTERNAL AREA: 616 SQ M
IMAGES: GEORGE DUPIN

The difficult brief called for an extension to an orangery of uncertain age which impacted as little as possible on the views from the main house and on the mature landscape in which it is set. This suggested the L-shaped general plan and the use of an indigenous stone for retaining walls. But it did not suggest half-burying a series of interconnecting cave-like rooms nor the five three storey board marked concrete towers that poke out of the rockery-roof. This is where the ingenuity of the architect comes in. This is masterful house-making by an architect who has brought a little bit of San Gimignano to this corner of the Ile de France and made an originally sceptical client and his family more than happy.

Dune House
Aldeburgh Road, Thorpeness, Suffolk

JARMUND VIGSNÆS ARCHITECTS
AND MOLE ARCHITECTS

CLIENT: LIVING ARCHITECTURE
CONTRACTOR: WILLOW BUILDERS
STRUCTURAL ENGINEER: JANE WERNICK ASSOCIATES
CONTRACT VALUE: CONFIDENTIAL
DATE OF COMPLETION: DECEMBER 2010
GROSS INTERNAL AREA: 243 SQ M
IMAGES: CHRIS WRIGHT
LIVING ARCHITECTURE SHORTLISTED FOR RIBA CLIENT OF THE YEAR

Alain de Botton's Living Architecture concept allows people to find out what it is like to live in a fine piece of architecture, albeit for just a few days. While enjoying a pleasant holiday they might be taking their first steps to becoming clients themselves. This example, with Mole Architects again taking the executive architects role (as they did with another non UK firm MVRDV on the Balancing Barn), is a conceptually bold project that is also well-detailed and constructed. An open plan living space hunkered into its land is topped by four tent-like bedrooms above. Architecturally the roof form plays on the local vernacular gables and sheds but is also an exploration in geometry. The house achieves a 20% improvement in energy efficiency over current building regulations.

Private House
Gloucestershire

DAVID RUSSELL, FOUND ASSOCIATES

CLIENT: PRIVATE
STRUCTURAL ENGINEER: FJ SAMUELY
CONTRACTOR: HORGAN BROTHERS CONSTRUCTION
CONTRACT VALUE: CONFIDENTIAL
DATE OF COMPLETION: APRIL 2011
GROSS INTERNAL AREA: 472 SQ M
IMAGES: HUFTON + CROW (TOP; MIDDLE RIGHT);
DAVID RUSSELL (MIDDLE LEFT; BOTTOM)

The planners required that any new building on the site must be an extension to a tiny neglected gamekeeper's cottage and that it be subordinate to it in scale. End of project. Instead the architect and the client successfully argued for a series of dry stone walls and terraces in which the house is buried under grass roofs. The result is a house of substantial scale that does not overwhelm the cottage, with its linear form exploited to create an unfolding sequence of spaces of special character. This is a project of great simplicity, in terms of materials and strategy and at the same time, considerable sophistication, in its theatrical approach to space and light with both framed and expansive views and contrasting spatial events.

Private House
East Sussex

DUGGAN MORRIS ARCHITECTS

CLIENT: PRIVATE
STRUCTURAL ENGINEER: STEPHEN EVANS ASSOCIATES, BROOKS DEVLIN
CONTRACTOR: NORTHLAKE
CONTRACT VALUE: CONFIDENTIAL
DATE OF COMPLETION: FEBRUARY 2011
GROSS INTERNAL AREA: 433 SQ M
IMAGES: MARK HADDEN (TOP); JAMES BRITTAIN (BOTTOM)

The site is a mile from the nearest public road or neighbour. Even so a conflict between the needs of the client and the demands of conservation officials who wanted the replication of a traditional farm building aesthetic had to be brilliantly resolved by breaking up and burying part of the new building so it appears to be a collection of cellular timber outbuildings dominated by the bulk of the two oast-houses. Yet internally it is quite the reverse. The 'separate' barns form a beautiful continuous flowing open plan living area linking into bedrooms in the restored oasthouses. The polished concrete floor and kitchen island coupled with the large sliding glass wall to the semi-sunken garden give an almost opulent effect to the whole.

Two Passive Solar Gain Houses in Porthtowan

Porthtowan, Truro, Cornwall

SIMON CONDER ASSOCIATES

CLIENT: PRIVATE
STRUCTURAL ENGINEER: FLUID STRUCTURES
CONTRACTOR: T&D CARTER
CONTRACT VALUE: £928,158
DATE OF COMPLETION: FEBRUARY 2012
GROSS INTERNAL AREA: 327 SQ M
IMAGES: PAUL SMOOTHY

These sibling houses are located high on a headland with stunning views out to sea. Clad entirely in timber, including the flat roofs, they are created out of a strong, simple and confident diagram, and are immaculately detailed. A skilful manipulation of plan and section ensures that all main spaces benefit from the expansive views. Built into the 1 in 7 slope, the site establishes a simple, successful passive sustainable approach: thermal mass, solar gain and natural ventilation each being exploited, with no sense of claustrophobia resulting from the semi-buried forms. With very low energy consumption, consistent, elegant detailing and construction, these houses are great examples of how thoughtful, modest and economic architecture can create a passive sustainable living environment.

THE STEPHEN LAWRENCE PRIZE

SPONSORED BY THE MARCO GOLDSCHMIED FOUNDATION

THE WINNER
KING'S GROVE
LONDON
Duggan Morris Architects

THE SHORTLIST
DELLOW DAY CENTRE
LONDON
Featherstone Young

HILL TOP HOUSE
OXFORD
Adrian James Architects

PRIVATE HOUSE
KENT
Hampson Williams Architects

THE MARQUIS HOTEL & RESTAURANT
KENT
Guy Holloway Architects

Established in 1998 in memory of the murdered black teenager who aspired to be an architect, this prize rewards the best examples of projects with a construction budget of less than £1 million. The award is judged by Marco Goldschmied, Phil Coffey and Doreen Lawrence OBE.

The Stephen Lawrence Prize was set up in 1998 to draw attention to the Stephen Lawrence Trust to assist young black students to study architecture and to reward smaller projects and the creativity required when architects are working with low budgets.

THE JUDGES
MARCO GOLDSCHMIED
PHIL COFFEY
DOREEN LAWRENCE OBE

King's Grove
London SE15

DUGGAN MORRIS ARCHITECTS

CLIENT: PRIVATE
STRUCTURAL ENGINEER: LYONS O'NEIL
SERVICES ENGINEER: BROOKS DEVILN
CONTRACTOR: ME CONSTRUCTION
CONTRACT VALUE: £320,000
DATE OF COMPLETION: JULY 2010
GROSS INTERNAL AREA: 140 SQ M
IMAGES: EDMUND SUMNER (TOP); JAMES BRITTAIN (BOTTOM LEFT);
MARK HADDEN (BOTTOM RIGHT)

The judges were entranced by the demure entrance to this new build all-brick house in the back lands of two Victorian terraces in Peckham. The architects had to deal with local residents, party wall agreements and the local planning department to come up with a home that, inside and out, is practical, simple, subtle, timeless and elegant. The house is arranged with ground floor living spaces connected to the two bedrooms by means of a simple stair and a central light-well. The maturity in layout and detailing is evident throughout, not least in the striking bespoke brass window frames recessed into the front and rear façades. Despite this being a home for the architects themselves, there is little sign of the architect … but plenty of architecture.

Dellow Day Centre
Wentworth Street, London E1

FEATHERSTONE YOUNG

CLIENT: PROVIDENCE ROW
STRUCTURAL ENGINEER: CONISBEE
ENVIRONMENTAL ENGINEER: FES (FUTURE ENERGY SURVEYS)
CONTRACTOR: JOHN PERKINS PROJECTS
CONTRACT VALUE: CONFIDENTIAL
DATE OF COMPLETION: NOVEMBER 2011
GROSS INTERNAL AREA: 366 SQ M
IMAGES: TIM BROTHERTON

This new building inserted into a narrow gap within the densely packed buildings and streets around Whitechapel provides workshop, studio, storage and office facilities for a charity working with homeless people. The new accommodation is arranged over three floors that look across a small courtyard to the charity's existing day centre. The ground floor contains the workshop space with doors opening onto the courtyard, allowing activities and events to use and animate the space. Enclosed on three sides, the new building effectively has a single elevation fronting on to a courtyard. The body of the building is clad in yellow and green coloured profiled steel panels with perforated screens. This project demonstrates the benefits that a creative design approach can bring even within a modest budget.

Hill Top House
Oxford

ADRIAN JAMES ARCHITECTS

CLIENT: PRIVATE
STRUCTURAL ENGINEER: PRICE & MYERS
CONTRACTOR: CARTER CONSTRUCTION
CONTRACT VALUE: CONFIDENTIAL
DATE OF COMPLETION: AUGUST 2011
GROSS INTERNAL AREA: 180 SQ M
IMAGES: DAVID FISCHER

The architects describe this scheme as 'an essay in concrete for clients who relish the uncompromising ascetic quality of the material'. The four-level house on the narrow site of a tumbledown garage is slotted in a terrace of Edwardian houses. It follows a rigorous plan with a compact central core zone housing the lateral in-situ concrete stairs and all services to bathrooms and kitchen with double volume corridor zones on either side. Despite the small footprint, the abiding impression is one of space flowing in all directions. The back wall is placed on a 45 degree diagonal made up of a double-height glass screen with the living room behind. It provides brilliant distant views of the centre of Oxford. Altogether a tour-de-force in urban residential design.

Private House
Ulcombe, Kent

HAMPSON WILLIAMS ARCHITECTS

CLIENT: PRIVATE
STRUCTURAL ENGINEER: WEBB YATES ENGINEERS
SERVICES ENGINEER: ENG DESIGN
CONTRACTOR: QUBE SPECIAL PROJECTS
CONTRACT VALUE: CONFIDENTIAL
DATE OF COMPLETION: FEBRUARY 2012
GROSS INTERNAL AREA: 335 SQ M
IMAGES: TIM SOAR

The brief called for a house that reflected the environmental
sensitivities of the client, was contemporary in design, honest
in its expression both of form and material and rooted in
place. As with all private houses the type of spaces and their
arrangement is intensely personal, and it requires sensitivity
on the part of the architect and openness on the part of the
client if the latter's wishes are to be fulfilled. Here the design
process was clearly an open, collaborative and flexible one.
The house was conceived as a primarily timber construction.
By using re-cycled excavation material as a retaining wall the
carbon footprint was kept low and the project on came in on
budget.

The Marquis Hotel & Restaurant
Alkham, Dover, Kent

GUY HOLLAWAY ARCHITECTS

CLIENT: PRIVATE
STRUCTURAL ENGINEERS: A J LOCKE CONSULTING ENGINEERS
SERVICES ENGINEERS: BRYANT AND REINA GROUP
CONTRACTOR: GSE DESIGN AND BUILD
CONTRACT VALUE: CONFIDENTIAL
DATE OF COMPLETION: NOVEMBER 2011
GROSS INTERNAL AREA: 235 SQ M
IMAGES: ASHLEY GENDEK

The Grade II Listed boutique hotel had previously been refurbished by the same architects. Due to the success of the scheme and of the restaurant, 'The Marquis' has now had to be extended to provide additional hotel rooms, improved staff facilities and an enlarged kitchen. The low lying, simply built form of the new building replaces an existing cottage on the steep site and can be read individually, so that it has minimal impact on the nearby church. It is tied into its surroundings with the use of locally sourced flint and Kent Peg Tiles reclaimed from the demolished cottage and a sedum roof meshes it into the landscape. This is a fine example of good architecture engendering business success.

THE RIBA CLIENT OF THE YEAR

SUPPORTED BY THE BLOXHAM CHARITABLE TRUST

THE WINNER

OLYMPIC DELIVERY AUTHORITY AND LONDON ORGANISING COMMITTEE OF THE OLYMPIC GAMES
for the London Olympic Stadium and 40 other buildings

Since 1998 the RIBA has recognised the role good clients play in the delivery of fine architecture. The award is judged by Tom Bloxham MBE and the RIBA Awards Group.

THE SHORTLIST

ARGENT
for Phase 1: Granary Complex, Central Saint Martin's at King's Cross by Stanton Williams and previous award winner Brindleyplace, Birmingham by various architects

LIVING ARCHITECTURE
for The Dune House by Jarmund Vigsnæs Architects and Mole Architects and previous award winners Balancing Barn (2011) and Shingle House (2011)

MANHATTAN LOFT CORPORATION
for St Pancras Chambers by RHWL Architects and Richard Griffiths Architects

WAKEFIELD COUNCIL
for Hepworth Wakefield by David Chipperfield Architects, Sandal Magna Community Primary School by Sarah Wigglesworth Architects and Castleford Bridge, Castleford Project by McDowell + Benedetti (2009)

OLYMPIC DELIVERY AUTHORITY
AND LONDON ORGANISING COMMITTEE
OF THE OLYMPIC GAMES

The Olympic Delivery Authority and their successors the
London Organising Committee of the Olympic Games
have delivered what is probably the greatest architectural
commission ever in this country. They selected 41 firms,
all by competition, from major practices such as Hopkins
and Populous, to small ones like Pernilla and Asif with their
interactive Beat Box.

    The mammoth, hugely popular and successful enterprise
was led by project sponsor Ian Crockford and Design principal
Kevin Owens, whose energy and enthusiasm inspired the
design and construction team to work in a seamlessly
collaborative manner to an unprecedentedly challenging
programme.

    The result was a series of some spectacular but all highly
functional venues, seen across the world by hundreds of
millions of people – the biggest ever audience for great
architecture. What is more they have delivered a sustainable
legacy for years to come.

IMAGE: LONDON 2012

ARGENT

Stanton Williams have had a close and constructive relationship with Argent since working with them at Brindley Place, Birmingham. As the client for a new campus building for Central St Martin's at King's Cross, they have continued to value dialogue and shown a genuine commitment to raising the benchmark, both in terms of the construction process and design quality. In an industry that is constantly under pressure to deliver projects on time and on budget, Argent remain an extremely supportive and stimulating company to work with.

IMAGE: HUFTON + CROW

LIVING ARCHITECTURE

Living Architecture are the kind of clients architects dreams of. They don't just appoint internationally respected architects and give them free rein: the reality is slightly different, and infinitely better. Living Architecture are not only supportive and appreciative of the ideas of their architects, they are also demanding, attentive and interested in the finest details. Rarely is an architect interrogated to secure both intellectual rigour and practicality every step along the way; the buildings are all the better as a result of this process.

IMAGE: CHRIS WRIGHT

MANHATTAN LOFT CORPORATION

Manhattan Lofts were appointed in 1997 to convert St Pancras Chambers into a hotel and residential apartments. Undaunted by the iconic status of one of the most famous historic buildings of the nineteenth century, MD Harry Handlesman appointed an experienced design team to restore, convert and extend the buildings to provide sufficient hotel bedrooms for viability, and to negotiate the works past the close scrutiny of English Heritage. The result – in the teeth of recession – is a commercial and architectural triumph.

IMAGE: HUFTON + CROW

WAKEFIELD COUNCIL

The ambition of Wakefield Council to develop not only the Hepworth gallery, but also the waterfront area, is immense. Led by John Foster, Wakefield's then chief executive, and project director Gordon Watson the Council drew up a brief that demanded a design of the very highest standard.

Wakefield is a serially good client, with a series of other fine commissions: Sarah Wigglesworth's Stirling-midlisted Sandal Magna School, and the Castleford Project, a series of public works and buildings whose centre-piece was the bridge by McDowell and Benedetti which won the RIBA/CABE public space award.

IMAGE: IWAN BAAN

THE RIBA AWARDS

The RIBA Awards were established in 1966 to reward the architects and clients of the UK's best buildings. Juries are asked to judge the quality of the design of the scheme particularly in respect of: sustainability, budget, the spatial experience it offers, the complexity of brief / degree of difficulty, its architectural ambition and ideas, its design vision, the selection and detailing of materials, the extent of innovation/ invention/originality, the contract type, the appropriateness of its structural and servicing systems, its fitness for purpose, especially in response to the client's brief as reflected in the level of client satisfaction, its response to the issues of accessibility and other social factors and its capacity to stimulate, engage and delight its occupants and visitors. They are reminded that an award-winning project should be capable of enduring as a fine work of architecture throughout its working life.

The RIBA's awards system was overhauled in 2012, so that architects enter one set of awards, where previously they were required to enter at national and regional level (see page 138 for RIBA Regional Awards). All entries are first visited by a local architect to see if they merit a visit from a full regional jury of three, consisting of an architect chair from outside the region, one from that region and a 'lay' juror, such as an engineer, client, artist or journalist. These juries agree RIBA Regional Awards and make strong recommendations to the national Awards Group on RIBA Awards. Both sets of awards are presented in the RIBA regions.

THE JUDGES

The regional judges are listed in the following order: chair, regional representative and lay assessor

Scotland

SHOLTO HUMPHRIES
ROBERT DYE
  (RIBA REPRESENTATIVE)
PETER WILSON/DR ANNE
LORNE GILLIES

Northern Ireland

RUTH REED
STEVEN SPIER
WILLIAM CRAWLEY

North-East

ANTHONY HUDSON
ERIC CARTER
CHRIS BROWN

North-West

MICHAEL SQUIRE
ANDY AVERY
NICOLE CROCKETT

Yorkshire

JULIAN MARSH
SIMON BAKER
KESTER RATTENBURY

Wales

STEPHEN HODDER
DOUG HUGHES
CAROLE-ANNE-DAVIES

West Midlands

PIERRE WASSENAAR
KEVIN SINGH
JAY MERRICK

East Midlands

CHARLIE HUSSEY
MARK JERMY
PETER WILSON

East

ANNA LIU
ROGER SHRIMPLIN
MATT JONES

South-West and Wessex

STUART MCKNIGHT
DAVID SHEPPARD/DAVID
MELLOR
ANDREW GRANT

South

MARCO GOLDSCHMIED
WARREN WHYTE
ALICIA PIVARO

South-East

MARCO GOLDSCHMIED
JAMES GALPIN
ALICIA PIVARO/MARTIN
QUALTERS

London East

GARETH HOSKINS
PAUL KARAKUSEVIC
RORY OLCAYTO

London North

SIMON HENLEY
LARS TEICHMANN
CLIVE DUTTON

London South

PATTY HOPKINS
JONATHAN LEAH
JEREMY TITCHEN

London West

DENISE BENNETTS
JOE MORRIS
RICHARD SIMMONS

Bogbain Mill
Lochussie, by Maryburgh

RURAL DESIGN

CLIENT: PRIVATE
CONTRACT VALUE: CONFIDENTIAL
DATE OF COMPLETION: 2011
GROSS INTERNAL AREA: 350 SQ M
IMAGES: ANDREW LEE

With this re-working of an old stone mill the architect has
created a number of simple timber pavilions and additions
to the 'found' walls, threading through cross-axes and
arranged in unfolding layers over the ruins to create a series
of courtyards. The old stone mill with its new interventions is
punctured by a secluded private entrance to the main living
wing, whilst rising to a three-storey larch-clad prow looking out
to the wood. A glass-sided cube pushes out through the old
L-plan into a second open-ended courtyard. Everywhere, there
is natural light and framed views. The old fabric is preserved
and, with the oak structure is revealed inside the main living
wing in a conscious, clear manner. This is sustainable domestic
architecture of high quality, imagination and clarity.

Dundee House

REIACH AND HALL ARCHITECTS

CLIENT: DUNDEE CITY COUNCIL
STRUCTURAL ENGINEER: BURO HAPPOLD
SERVICES ENGINEER: BURO HAPPOLD
CONTRACTOR: BOVIS LEND LEASE
CONTRACT VALUE: £29.85 MILLION
DATE OF COMPLETION: JULY 2011
GROSS INTERNAL AREA: 12,078 SQ M
IMAGES: DAVE MORRIS PHOTOGRAPHY

Set within a previously run down part of the city centre, this building, which combines an historic printing works with an HQ for the City Council, is designed as a catalyst for new development. Behind the historic façade are set seven storeys of modern office space. The access spines on each floor, in unembellished concrete signal the transition from the historic to the new, generating an easily understood and navigated internal layout. Large open plan floor plates, interspersed with breakout areas and lightwells, encourage cross-disciplinary working. The new structure maximises natural lighting while the window reveals reduce heat gain. The treatment of the tripartite rear elevation is human in scale. Its contemporary classicism is a foil to the Edwardian historic frontage.

National Museum of Scotland
Chambers Street, Edinburgh

GARETH HOSKINS ARCHITECTS

CLIENT: NATIONAL MUSEUMS OF SCOTLAND
STRUCTURAL ENGINEER: DAVID NARRO ASSOCIATES
SERVICES ENGINEER: MAX FORDHAM
CONTRACTOR: BALFOUR BEATTY CONSTRUCTION
CONTRACT VALUE: £47.4 MILLION
DATE OF COMPLETION: JULY 2011
GROSS INTERNAL AREA: 30,000 SQ M
IMAGES: ANDREW LEE

The completion of the second phase of the masterplan has expanded the gallery spaces, restored much of the original architect's intent and significantly improved access and visitor facilities. The main façade has been opened up to create new accessible street level entrances, the existing basement stores have been excavated to form a new entrance hall with shop and café, and new staircases and lifts to the refurbished 'grand gallery'. This transformed museum now fully merits its national epithet. All the big moves are deftly delivered. This adaptation is sensitive and intelligent, enhancing both the building and the objects displayed within it. Fully accessible with a welcoming new ground floor entrance, the whole design encourages visitors to see every part of this important collection.

Scottish National Portrait Gallery
Edinburgh

PAGE\PARK ARCHITECTS

CLIENT: NATIONAL GALLERIES OF SCOTLAND
STRUCTURAL ENGINEER: WILL RUDD DAVIDSON
SERVICES ENGINEER: HARLEY HADDOW
CONTRACTOR: BAM
CONTRACT VALUE: £11.5 MILLION
DATE OF COMPLETION: JULY 2011
GROSS INTERNAL AREA: 30,000 SQ. M
IMAGES: ANDREW LEE

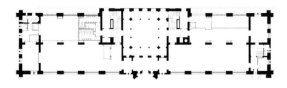

This is a highly intelligent re-organisation and re-working of an old facility that although held in nostalgic affection had been fundamentally flawed in use since its inception. The architects have added discreet access ramps and made two new openings into the enormous linear entrance hall. The insertion of a glass lift and mezzanine reorganises the space into a legible *en-filade* sequence. The new lift takes the visitor directly to all of the floors including the previously undernourished top galleries, while the mezzanine both unlocks space and solves the problems of fire escape. The pay-off for these alterations is a series of five interlinked, soaring roof-lit galleries on the top floor, which significantly increase the quality and quantity of first-class wall hanging space.

Osborne Park Extension and Refurbishment

Osborne Park, Belfast

ARD (CIARAN MACKEL) ARCHITECTS

CLIENT: MR AND MRS T LACY
STRUCTURAL ENGINEER: DESIGN ID
CONTRACTOR: CANAVAN CONSTRUCTION LTD
CONTRACT VALUE: CONFIDENTIAL
IMAGES: AIDAN MONAGHAN PHOTOGRAPHY/FEARGHAL MURRAY

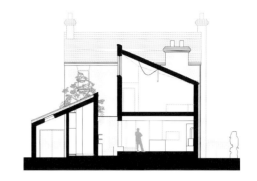

This major addition to a double-bay, detached Victorian villa, is tucked away from the street and is seen in the context of the rear off-shots and extensions of suburban Belfast. The composition of gabled extensions remains sympathetic to the varied rear treatments acquired by neighbouring properties over the years. The rationalisation of the functions, spaces and detailing, however, are in marked contrast. Along the width of the house the distinction between served and servant spaces is articulated in massing and materials. The two activities are separated by a courtyard and an in-between space, these provide a discrete and stylish workplace in the heart of the family home. The new spaces bring light into the depth of the plan balancing the formal Victorian rooms at the front of the house.

Glenariffe House
Glens of Antrim

MCGARRY – MOON ARCHITECTS

CLIENT: PRIVATE
STRUCTURAL ENGINEER: AECOM
CONTRACTOR: DERMOT MCMULLAN
CONTRACT VALUE: CONFIDENTIAL
IMAGES: STEVEN MOON

Set within the Glens of Antrim on the side of the valley running down to the sea, this house respects the rural architecture of the area while providing an immaculately detailed modern interpretation of a country home with excellent environmental credentials. From the road the massing and white rendered exterior refers directly to the rural vernacular without pastiche. Beyond the entrance elevation the house terraces down the steep site through single and double height spaces clearly articulated in the external massing. Internally the space flows though the living spaces and the proportion and placement of windows allow stunning views while allowing one to feel contained. With its response to topography and architectural context this is a place of and in the landscape.

Public Record Office of Northern Ireland (PRONI)
Belfast

TODD ARCHITECTS

CLIENT: TITANIC QUARTER LTD
STRUCTURAL ENGINEER: RPS CONSULTING ENGINEERS, BELFAST
SERVICES ENGINEER: DELAP & WALLER
CONTRACTOR: HARCOURT CONSTRUCTION (NI) LTD
CONTRACT VALUE: CONFIDENTIAL
IMAGES: CHRIS HILL

EAST ELEVATION

This concrete citadel is a repository of history and is clearly but unobtrusively organised in its functions of collection, preservation, storage and access. The abundance of natural light and the calm, polished feel of the interior lend it an inviting yet hushed air. Some buildings contain art, others incorporate art. PRONI's ambitious new building integrates art both externally and internally in a quiet way that serves the building's function as a repository of memories. Not only is the building emphatically sustainable environmentally but it also treats this approach as a given by prioritising the quality of use, space and light. It suggests that the days of conflict between architectural quality and environmental sustainability are well behind us.

Information

Roseberry Park
Middlesbrough

MEDICAL ARCHITECTURE

CLIENT: TEES, ESK AND WEAR VALLEYS NHS FOUNDATION TRUST
STRUCTURAL ENGINEER: WSP GROUP
SERVICES ENGINEER: DESCO (DESIGN AND CONSULTANCY)
CONTRACTOR: LAING O'ROURKE CONSTRUCTION NORTH
CONTRACT VALUE: £75 MILLION
DATE OF COMPLETION: OCTOBER 2010
GROSS INTERNAL AREA: 27,034 SQ M
IMAGES: JILL TATE (TOP); CREDIT COLOUR UDL (CENTRE);
COLIN DAVISON (BOTTOM)
WINNER OF RIBA REGIONAL CLIENT OF THE YEAR AWARD

This is a large and ambitious project for a 312 bed mental health village undertaken under the Public Finance Initiative. This new building type is currently being reassessed by the NHS to see how they work for patients and staff. The village replaces an existing Victorian building that was clearly not suitable to either. The success of its replacement is demonstrated by the fact that one discharged patient ram-raided the gate to get back in. The staff also believe the buildings iron out potential flash points that can occur in the day-to-day care of patients. Overall there is a relaxed atmosphere with accommodation arranged around courtyards with varying degrees of security. Rooms are imaginatively designed to accommodate the psychological needs of the patients.

The Toffee Factory

Lower Steenberg's Yard, Quayside, Ouseburn,
Newcastle upon Tyne

XSITE ARCHITECTURE

CLIENT: 1NG
STRUCTURAL ENGINEER: CUNDALL
SERVICES ENGINEER: MAX FORDHAM
CONTRACTOR: BRIMS CONSTRUCTION
CONTRACT VALUE: £4.9 MILLION
DATE OF COMPLETION: DECEMBER 2011
GROSS INTERNAL: 2,682 SQ M
IMAGES: JILL TATE
WINNER OF RIBA REGIONAL SUSTAINABILITY AWARD AND
BUILDING OF THE YEAR AWARD

The derelict toffee factory, with a forest of trees growing out
of its ruined shell, has been reincarnated as managed work
space for the creative industries and is almost fully let. It has
become a landmark in the regeneration of the Ouseburn
Valley and a significant addition to Newcastle's architectural
legacy. The original building fabric has been restored
including the distinctive chimney and an additional floor
has been added. The demands of energy conservation have
led to an interesting chequerboard of insulation alternating
between inside and out, so one is always aware of the original
structure. The insertion of a first floor external walkway, which
plays on the industrial heritage, removes the necessity of
a third fire escape staircase. The building has achieved a
BREEAM Very Good rating.

Brockholes Visitor Centre
Preston New Road, Samlesbury, Preston

ADAM KHAN ARCHITECTS

CLIENT: LANCASHIRE WILDLIFE TRUST
STRUCTURAL ENGINEER: PRICE AND MYERS
SERVICES ENGINEER: MAX FORDHAM
CONTRACTOR: MANSELL CONSTRUCTION SERVICES LIMITED
CONTRACT VALUE: £6.25 MILLION
DATE OF COMPLETION: MAY 2011
GROSS INTERNAL AREA: 1,400 SQ M
IMAGES: IOANA MARINESCU
WINNER OF RIBA REGIONAL SUSTAINABILITY AWARD
WINNER OF RIBA REGIONAL BUILDING OF THE YEAR AWARD
MIDLISTED FOR RIBA STIRLING PRIZE

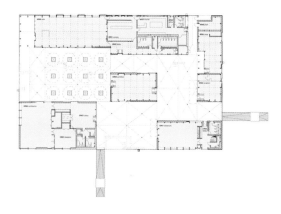

The visitor centre at Brockholes is a cluster of buildings set in a lake on a floating pontoon, which responds to changing water levels in the flood plain. The architect has broken down what is a sizeable scheme into a simple and engaging village of buildings – restaurant, a shop, an exhibition hall, an education centre and a conference centre – designed to celebrate the natural environment. Each cube or rectangle of accommodation has a barn-like roof creating an animated skyline floating above the lake. What is most impressive is that here is a romantic conceptual idea, underpinned by sustainability, structural integrity, function and detail. A natural ventilation system is discreetly integrated, exploiting the stack effect of the barn-shaped roofs, resulting in a BREEAM Excellent rating.

Festival House
Promenade, Blackpool

dRMM ARCHITECTS
CLIENT: BLACKPOOL COUNCIL
CONTRACTOR: PARKINSON BUILDING CONTRACTORS
STRUCTURAL ENGINEER: MICHAEL HADI ASSOCIATES
SERVICES ENGINEER: MICHAEL POPPER ASSOCIATES
CONTRACT VALUE: CONFIDENTIAL
DATE OF COMPLETION: DECEMBER 2011
GROSS INTERNAL AREA: 565 SQ M
IMAGES: ALEX DE RIJKE; CHRIS ASTBURY (BOTTOM RIGHT)

Blackpool is a town in need of regeneration, and a key to achieving this is building upon the history of the town's identity as a centre for entertainment and vacation. The building provides a restaurant and tourist information centre at promenade level, on the first floor is a registry office, and above that is a wedding ceremony hall with a precisely framed view of Blackpool Tower. The structure consists of pre-fabricated cross-laminated timber panels manufactured off site. This is clad in golden stainless steel shingles above a plinth clad in stepped concrete blocks containing recycled and phosphorescent glass which catches the light. The project has achieved a BREEAM bespoke rating of Excellent, with very low air permeability and maximised access to daylight reducing energy consumption.

North House
Bowden

ROGER STEPHENSON ARCHITECTS

CLIENT: PRIVATE
STRUCTURAL ENGINEER: DEAKIN WALTON
SERVICES ENGINEER: NORMAN DISNEY YOUNG
CONTRACTOR: ERIC WRIGHT CONSTRUCTION
CONTRACT VALUE: CONFIDENTIAL
DATE OF COMPLETION: JANUARY 2010
GROSS INTERNAL AREA: 560 SQ M
IMAGES: DANIEL HOPKINSON

North House is a substantial detached family home in a street of impressive Victorian villas and is an example of how an uncompromisingly contemporary house can sit comfortably and calmly in a conservation area and its existence is due to a sympathetic planning officer who recognised on appeal the sensitivity of the composition. Despite the affluent nature of this new family home, there is a modesty about the materials and a subtlety to the technology which together deliver a comfortable and sustainable house. The organisation of the building exploits the topography of the site, producing great views. The house includes accommodation for an elderly relative which is designed to ensure accessibility from the street and also via a ramp to the gardens.

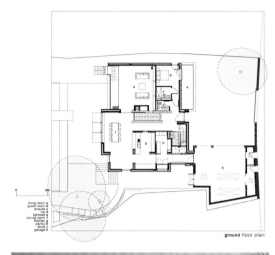

living room a
guest room b
ensuite c
wc d
lightwell e
dining room f
kitchen g
pantry h
store i
garage j

ground floor plan

Kirk Balk Community College
Hoyland, Barnsley

ALLFORD HALL MONAGHAN MORRIS
CLIENT: BARNSLEY METROPOLITAN BOROUGH COUNCIL
STRUCTURAL ENGINEER: BURO HAPPOLD
SERVICES ENGINEER: BDP
CONTRACTOR: LAING O'ROURKE
CONTRACT VALUE: £18.58 MILLION
DATE OF COMPLETION: APRIL 2011
GROSS INTERNAL AREA: 11,877 SQ M
IMAGES: TIMOTHY SOAR
WINNER OF RIBA REGIONAL CLIENT OF THE YEAR AWARD

Aware of the wilful form-making that has characterised a large number of Building Schools for the Future projects, the architects proposed a solution that comprised of two simple geometric forms, a triangle and a rectangle. In the wrong hands this approach could have been leaden, here it is endlessly subtle. The sloping hilltop site is cleverly used to generate complex, often top-lit, interior spaces with exceptional views. This is all enabled by the large space at the centre of the triangular form which gives a very high level of visual inter-connectedness. Corridors always end in a view and corners of the triangle are cut out to make viewing places and unexpected places turned into unexpected vistas.

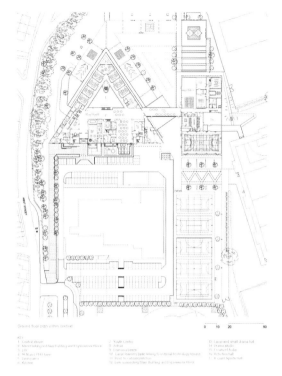

Ground floor plan within context

Saxton
The Avenue, Leeds

UNION NORTH

CLIENT: URBAN SPLASH
STRUCTURAL ENGINEER: ARUP
SERVICES ENGINEER: ARUP
CONTRACTOR: URBAN SPLASH BUILD
CONTRACT VALUE: £40 MILLION
DATE OF COMPLETION: JULY 2011
GROSS INTERNAL AREA: 25,232 SQ M
IMAGES: JOEL FILDES
WINNER OF RIBA REGIONAL SUSTAINABILITY AWARD

This refurbishment of two derelict council housing blocks offers a paradigm for regeneration in these straightened times that combines both social and environmental sustainability. Intensive consultation has led to a genuinely mixed-tenure scheme, with the number of homes on the site rising from 214 to 410 – apartments are small, but light and cheerful, with spectacular views. The existing structure, lifts and stairs have been re-used, adding to the outside a new steel structure to provide the increased density and allow the building to be clad in a highly insulating but very elegant new skin. The sloping site was cleverly used to separate out the social heart from the ubiquitous parking areas and to make a communal entrance with a strong relationship back to the city.

Maggie's South West Wales
Singleton Hospital, Swansea

KISHO KUROKAWA ARCHITECT & ASSOCIATES
WITH GARBERS & JAMES

CLIENT: MAGGIE'S
STRUCTURAL ENGINEER: ARUP
SERVICES ENGINEER: KJ TAIT
CONTRACTOR: SIR ROBERT MCALPINE
CONTRACT VALUE: CONFIDENTIAL
DATE OF COMPLETION: DECEMBER 2011
GROSS INTERNAL AREA: 302 SQ M
IMAGES: THORE GARBERS

Kisho Kurokawa gifted the concept sketch for this Maggie's
Centre before his death in 2007. The ensuing design
presented a challenge to the architects tasked with delivering
the sketch in that the complex geometries had not been
defined. The outcome is a special and glorious little building
in many ways. The established programme of the Maggie's
Centres, the social kitchen and dining space at a pivotal
location in the building, is articulated beautifully in the plan
diagram and the architectural form. Externally, the standing
seam roof, which spirals and twists, prescribes the building's
form so appropriately. The concrete is of remarkable quality,
with embedded titanium plates that glisten in the sunlight.
This is a worthy addition to the spirit of Maggie's.

Royal Welsh College of Music and Drama
North Road, Cardiff

BFLS
CLIENT: ROYAL WELSH COLLEGE OF MUSIC AND DRAMA
STRUCTURAL ENGINEER: MOTT MACDONALD
SERVICES ENGINEER: MOTT MACDONALD
CONTRACTOR: WILMOTT DIXON CONSTRUCTION
CONTRACT VALUE: £15.75 MILLION
DATE OF COMPLETION: JUNE 2011
GROSS INTERNAL AREA: 4500 SQ M
IMAGES: NICK GUTTRIDGE
WINNER OF THE RIBA WELSH BUILDING OF THE YEAR AWARD
+ RIBA WELSH CLIENT OF THE YEAR AWARD

The Royal Welsh College of Music and Drama is Wales's national music and drama conservatoire. Despite the constraints of a tight site, the architects have created a new civic landmark for Cardiff. The building comprises the exquisitely timber-lined 450 seat Dora Stoutzker Concert Hall, the intimate 200-seat Richard Burton Theatre, along with studio, teaching, rehearsal spaces and café. The foyer has become one of the most popular community spaces in Cardiff where students, staff and the public meet. Between the new and existing buildings is a top-lit, triple height street, the Linbury Gallery. The building achieves BREEAM Excellent standard. The environmental strategy capitalises on the building's inherent thermal mass to naturally temper extremes in temperature.

BFI Master Film Store
Nr Gaydon

EDWARD CULLINAN ARCHITECTS

CLIENT: BRITISH FILM INSTITUTE
STRUCTURAL ENGINEER: CURTINS CONSULTING
SERVICES ENGINEER: COUCH PERRY & WILKES
CONTRACTOR: GILBERT ASH
CONTRACT VALUE: £9 MILLION
DATE OF COMPLETION: SEPTEMBER 2011
GROSS INTERNAL AREA: 2,900 SQ M
IMAGES: EDMUND SUMNER
WINNER OF RIBA REGIONAL BUILDING OF THE YEAR AWARD

This building might be described as a Modernist machine for preserving culture. The film stores protect 190,000 canisters of unstable nitrate film, and 240,000 acetate reels at minus 5°C, and at a fixed humidity. The archive could have been a simple response to functional imperatives – a serviceable oblong of concrete bunkers equating form with function – but this is more ambitious: a matrix of concrete bunkers clad with corrugated stainless steel; a distinct, characterful piece of architecture. In plan, elevations and material detailing, the Archive's design draws from both a stripped down industrial modernism, yet also radiates a very particular kind of twenty-first century finesse and environmental efficiency. The Archive is exemplary in both architectural and cultural terms.

Caistor Arts and Heritage Centre
Plough Hill, Caistor, Lincolnshire

JONATHAN HENDRY ARCHITECTS

CLIENT: CAISTOR ART & HERITAGE
STRUCTURAL ENGINEER: ALAN WOOD & PARTNERS
CONTRACTOR: WILTON COBLEY
CONTRACT VALUE: £348,000
DATE OF COMPLETION: APRIL 2011
GROSS INTERNAL AREA: 260 SQ M
IMAGES: DAVID GRANDORGE

The project to convert a dilapidated Methodist Chapel into
an Arts and Heritage Centre was the initiative of a group
of local people looking for a place to house a collection of
local artefacts. The closure of the library and the potential
for a small gallery and cafe changed the brief to one for a
new social hub for the village. All spaces are unified by a
simple black lacquered dado which changes according to
requirements – from plain wall panelling to storage for books
to display cabinets for the local historical artefacts. The
detailing is simple, well made and deeply considered and
the overall impression is both restrained but welcoming – a
delightful experience.

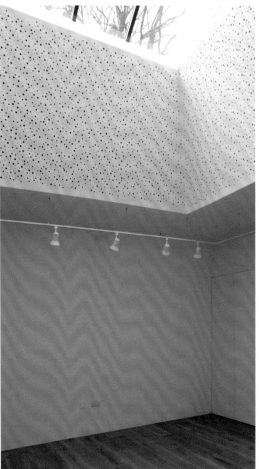

Easton Neston
Towcester, Northamptonshire

PTOLEMY DEAN ARCHITECTS

CLIENT: MAX STUDIO UK
STRUCTURAL ENGINEER: THE MORTON PARTNERSHIP
SERVICES ENGINEER: MICHAEL CADE ASSOCIATES
CONTRACTOR: BENNIE HISTORIC CONSERVATION
CONTRACT VALUE: CONFIDENTIAL
DATE OF COMPLETION: 2011
GROSS INTERNAL AREA: 4,616 SQ M
IMAGES: PTOLEMY DEAN ARCHITECTS
WINNER OF RIBA REGIONAL CONSERVATION AWARD

Easton Neston is one of the finest country houses in England, designed by Hawksmoor with an adjacent wing by Wren. Unsympathetic additions and a fire in 2002 meant there was much for the new owners and their architects to address. The historic setting clarified and repairs completed, attention turned to the sensitive incorporation of modern facilities to meet the needs of the Client's domestic and business requirements (which required the incorporation of his fashion studios and workshops). This has clearly been a labour of love for the past seven years, to return a wonderful piece of architecture to its former glory. The project has not only demanded a deep understanding of traditional craft, but also the ability to reconcile the demands of conservation with those of contemporary life.

Loughborough Design School
Towers Way, Loughborough, Leicestershire

BURWELL DEAKINS ARCHITECTS

CLIENT: LOUGHBOROUGH UNIVERSITY
STRUCTURAL ENGINEER: PRICE & MYERS
SERVICES ENGINEER: HOARE LEA
CONTRACTOR: SHEPHERD CONSTRUCTION
CONTRACT VALUE: £14.5 MILLION
DATE OF COMPLETION: SEPTEMBER 2011
GROSS INTERNAL AREA: 7,920 SQ M
IMAGES: HUFTON + CROW
WINNER OF RIBA REGIONAL CLIENT OF THE YEAR AWARD
+ RIBA REGIONAL SUSTAINABILITY AWARD
+ RIBA REGIONAL BUILDING OF THE YEAR AWARD

This is a 7,920 square metre building comprising teaching spaces, research laboratories, workshops, computer suites, offices and cafe, and is located within the existing university campus. It is a deep plan building on a roughly triangular footprint. Environmentally the inclusion of chimneys within the heart of the deep plan has helped the building to achieve a BREEAM Excellent rating. Structurally, the choice of concrete works well, offering both a robust and beautiful quality of finish to the interior spaces. Overall what impresses is the quality of natural daylight, the ease of circulation through the building, the integration of a simple but sophisticated approach to servicing and the overall quality of materials and attention to detail – all on a quite modest budget.

Brentwood School 6th Form & Assembly Hall

Ingrave Road, Brentwood, Essex

COTTRELL & VERMEULEN ARCHITECTURE

CLIENT: BRENTWOOD SCHOOL
STRUCTURAL ENGINEER: HASKINS ROBINSON WATERS
SERVICES ENGINEER: MAX FORDHAM
CONTRACTOR: HUTTON CONSTRUCTION
CONTRACT VALUE: CONFIDENTIAL
DATE OF COMPLETION: JULY 2011
GROSS INTERNAL AREA: 2375 SQ M
IMAGES: PAUL RIDDLE

Three buildings celebrate the spirit of education, unfolding as a sequence of spaces for learning, socialising, and gathering: a new Sixth Form block, a remodelled Victorian vicarage, and a new assembly block which links to a sequence of other smaller external social areas. Admirable innovations include internal thermal chimneys in every classroom, natural ventilation panels next to windows, and pre-cast concrete panels used as formwork for the cast-in-situ concrete. Drawing inspiration from the existing Victorian vicarage, the new design is expressed in a language that is both contextual and contemporary. The sculpting of the roofs creates non-standard, domestic-scaled classrooms filled with natural light, reminiscent of the gabled roofs of the Victorian vicarage yet with an added measure of playfulness.

Royal Veterinary College Student Village
Hatfield

HAWKINS\BROWN

CLIENT: ROYAL VETERINARY COLLEGE
STRUCTURAL ENGINEER: ELLIOT WOOD PARTNERSHIP
SERVICES ENGINEER: MAX FORDHAM
CONTRACTOR: MORGAN SINDALL
CONTRACT VALUE: CONFIDENTIAL
DATE OF COMPLETION: JANUARY 2011
GROSS INTERNAL AREA: 6,427 SQ M
IMAGES: TIM CROCKER
WINNER OF RIBA REGIONAL EDUCATION AWARD

Architecturally the buildings embody the concept of
sharing in a variety of ways. They thus celebrate not only
economy but the spirit of education, which best derives from
spontaneous meetings, interaction, and gathering.
The arrangement of the eight dormitory buildings creates a
series of shared vistas and shared green commons across the
site, spaced out enough so as not to steal light from each
other. Every room has east and west aspects. For every group
of six dormitory rooms, there is a shared communal room
and kitchenette. Diverse cladding materials – brick, timber,
punched aluminium – are well-detailed and constructed,
resulting in visual coherence. Repetition of the same building
modules achieves economy without monotony, as each of the
courtyards has different orientations and therefore vistas.

Dyson Centre for Neonatal Care
Royal United Hospital, Combe Park, Bath

FEILDEN CLEGG BRADLEY STUDIOS

CLIENT: ROYAL UNITED HOSPITAL BATH NHS TRUST
STRUCTURAL ENGINEER: BURO HAPPOLD
SERVICES ENGINEER: BURO HAPPOLD
CONTRACTOR: VINCI CONSTRUCTION UK
CONTRACT VALUE: £3 MILLION
DATE OF COMPLETION: JULY 2011
GROSS INTERNAL AREA: 1,167 SQ M
IMAGES: CRAIG AUCKLAND FOTOHAUS
WINNER OF RIBA REGIONAL CLIENT OF THE YEAR AWARD

By selecting architects with no prior UK healthcare
experience, nor pre-conceptions, the client has introduced a
new vein of thought to their medical campus. A pioneering
holistic approach has created a low-carbon building in which
the careful use of materials, light and scale, together generate
a calm and caring atmosphere for the care of premature
and sick babies. The architect added extra spaces such
as shared bay window seats for parents, a small colourful
playroom space for visiting children and private garden
rooms – all demonstrating a deep understand of the needs
of the end user. The understated nature of the architecture
disguises real innovation, such as the use of exposed cross
laminated timber, bringing a tactile quality to a usually sterile
environment.

The Holburne Museum
Great Pulteney Street, Bath

ERIC PARRY ARCHITECTS

CLIENT: THE HOLBURNE MUSEUM
STRUCTURAL ENGINEER: MOMENTUM CONSULTING ENGINEERS
SERVICES ENGINEER: ATELIER TEN
CONTRACTOR: SIR ROBERT MCALPINE
CONTRACT VALUE: £7.15 MILLION
DATE OF COMPLETION: MAY 2011
GROSS INTERNAL AREA: 1,900 SQ M
IMAGES: HELENE BINET (TOP + MIDDLE); PAUL RIDDLE
WINNER OF RIBA REGIONAL BUILDING OF THE YEAR AWARD
MIDLISTED FOR RIBA STIRLING PRIZE

This intelligent project has recovered a lost connection
between the city and an eighteenth century pleasure garden.
Glimpsed from a distance through the trees, there is an
unexpected ethereal quality to the extension to the Museum.
The use of materials and layering to the façade, creates a
sophisticated play of shadows, light and reflection – beautiful
and unique, creating a building of true character, that is
underpinned by careful historical research and analysis
and very much of its site. This project is successful on a
number of architectural levels, from strategic, rational
architectural thought, to the developed layering of the
external expression. The resulting building demonstrates
a skilful architect, uncompromising in his clarity of thought
and contemporary idiom, able to respect and enhance this
protected environment.

The Triangle
Northern Road, Swindon

GLEN HOWELLS ARCHITECTS
CLIENT: HAB OAKUS
STRUCTURAL ENGINEER: CURTINS CONSULTING
CONTRACTOR: WILLMOTT DIXON
CONTRACT VALUE: £4.2 MILLION
DATE OF COMPLETION: SEPTEMBER 2011
GROSS INTERNAL AREA: 3,465 SQ M
IMAGES: PAUL RAFTERY
WINNER OF RIBA REGIONAL SUSTAINABILITY AWARD
MIDLISTED FOR RIBA STIRLING PRIZE

Through a series of quiet, considered moves, this project
has established itself as an exemplar for low cost,
environmentally responsible social housing, with higher
densities than the client expected. The houses are a
thoughtful re-interpretation of the terrace vernacular, making
the most of a limited palette of materials. The terrace
is articulated with chimney-like ventilation stacks, well-
proportioned windows and the use of gabions to modify the
visual impact of the car. The house plans are compact, yet
sectional heights are stretched and window cills dropped,
creating homes that feel surprisingly spacious. The balance
of public, communal and private spaces is one of the great
successes of the project and demonstrates the importance
of good public realm design in creating sustainable
communities and desirable places to live.

3 Bed House

Garsington Opera Pavilion
Wormsley Estate, Stokenchurch

ROBIN SNELL ASSOCIATES

CLIENT: GARSINGTON OPERA
CONTRACTOR: UNUSUAL RIGGING; BURO HAPPOLD; SOUND SPACE DESIGN;
IAIN MACKINTOSH; GARDINER & THEOBALD
CONSULTANTS: MOMENTUM
CONTRACT VALUE: £1.8 MILLION
DATE OF COMPLETION: MAY 2011
GROSS INTERNAL AREA: 20,655 SQ M
IMAGES: DENNIS GILBERT (TOP + BOTTOM RIGHT); RICHARD DAVIES (MIDDLE);
MIKE HOBAN (BOTTOM LEFT)
WINNER OF RIBA REGIONAL CLIENT OF THE YEAR AWARD (SOUTH)
MIDLISTED FOR RIBA STIRLING PRIZE

In the great English tradition of distrust of the new followed by rapid assimilation into permanency and subsequent listing, Garsington's design concept is driven by the need for it to be a completely demountable 600 seat 'temporary structure'. Although it is supposed to be taken down every Autumn, the landowner likes it so much he already suggested leaving it in place after the first season. Nonetheless, it is entirely designed out of transportable elements which require one cherry picker to lift into place in a short space of time. Transparent sail fabric and timber panels form the enclosure. The 'foyer' is open to the adjoining lake. Garsington is a great Fun Palace Cedric Price can now smile down on.

Shulman Lecture Theatre
Queen's College, Oxford

BGS ARCHITECTS

CLIENT: QUEEN'S COLLEGE, OXFORD
STRUCTURAL ENGINEER: PRICE AND MYERS
SERVICES ENGINEER: HOARE LEA
CONTRACTOR: KINGERLEE
CONTRACT VALUE: 3 MILLION
DATE OF COMPLETION: SEPTEMBER 2011
GROSS INTERNAL AREA: 3,506 SQ M
IMAGES: ADRIAN ARBIB
WINNER OF RIBA REGIONAL SUSTAINABILITY AWARD (SOUTH)

The Shulman Lecture Theatre is remarkable for its skilful combination of traditional materials with an uncompromisingly modern design. The subject of critical debate during its design stage, it has become an integral and much loved part of the college from the moment it opened. It is in demand every day and evening. The use of the elegant columns as vertical cantilevers allows the roof structure to be free of horizontal ties. The roof thus floats effortlessly above the external walls and all but disappears internally. Closing the electrically operated large timber louvres transforms the space into an intimate living room. The building conveys that rare quality of feeling as if it has always been there.

Somerville College
Student Accommodation
Woodstock Road, Oxford

NIALL MCLAUGHLIN ARCHITECTS

CLIENT: SOMERVILLE COLLEGE
STRUCTURAL ENGINEER: PRICE AND MYERS
SERVICES ENGINEER: HOARE LEA
CONTRACTOR: LAING O'ROURKE
CONTRACT VALUE: £8.5 MILLION
DATE OF COMPLETION: OCTOBER 2011
GROSS INTERNAL AREA: 2,595 SQ M
IMAGES: NICK KANE; NIALL MCLAUGHLIN ARCHITECTS (BOTTOM LEFT)

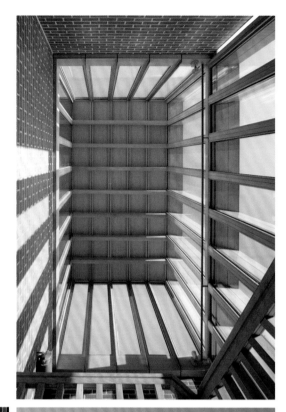

The demolition of the Radcliffe Infirmary exposed a blank façade as the college had long turned its back on the hospital. An exchange of land allowed a development on this edge site containing new student rooms and meaning the college can re-orientate its grounds towards a new Humanities faculty. Just six metres deep by 175 metres long the site is just big enough for a row of rooms with connecting corridor. Externally it creates one side of a new, yet to be completed street. The same architects have subsequently been commissioned to masterplan the empty site opposite, demonstrating how one job well done can so often lead to another.

McLaren Production Centre
Woking, Surrey

FOSTER + PARTNERS

CLIENT: MCLAREN GROUP
STRUCTURAL ENGINEER: BURO HAPPOLD
SERVICES ENGINEER: BURO HAPPOLD
CONTRACTOR: SIR ROBERT MCALPINE
CONTRACT VALUE: £35 MILLION
DATE OF COMPLETION: MAY 2011
GROSS INTERNAL AREA: 32,000 SQ M
IMAGES: MCLAREN MARKETING LTD (TOP); NIGEL YOUNG FOSTER + PARTNERS

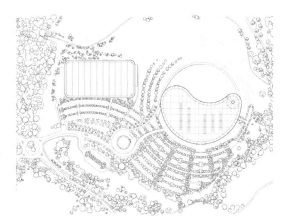

From the photos some might say: 'It's just a box', but that's like dismissing a Fabergé as 'just an egg'. The 300,000 cubic metre 'box' nestles successfully in the surrounding landscape. Quite an achievement in itself because few buildings convey so strongly, in their meticulous attention to every detail, the quality of the product being assembled within, and, in doing so, subtly contribute to selling it to the prospective purchaser of a McLaren. The long processional tunnel from the Technology Centre is Zen-like, devoid of any features or distractions. It allows the mind to focus on what is to come. The end of the journey is a blinding white empty curvilinear space reminiscent of a Godard film.

Turner Contemporary
Rendezvous, Margate, Kent

DAVID CHIPPERFIELD ARCHITECTS

CLIENT: KENT COUNTY COUNCIL
STRUCTURAL ENGINEER: ADAMS KARA TAYLOR
SERVICES ENGINEER: ARUP
CONTRACTOR: R DURTNELL & SONS
CONTRACT VALUE: £13.65 MILLION
DATE OF COMPLETION: DECEMBER 2010
GROSS INTERNAL AREA: 3,100 SQ M
IMAGES: RIDDLE-STAGG.COM (TOP); RICHARD BRYANT
WINNER OF RIBA REGIONAL BUILDING OF THE YEAR AWARD (SOUTH EAST)
MIDLISTED FOR RIBA STIRLING PRIZE

Deceptively simple, the Turner at Margate is a curator's dream. Ten years in the making from the Director's initial vision, it is a beautifully controlled sequence of galleries of a standard that has enabled the Turner Contemporary to exhibit material including works never previously seen by the public. Placed on the edge of the North Sea, the understated but carefully articulated white panelled exterior is unapologetically fortress-like and protective of the jewels within. The galleries skilfuilly combine natural and artificial lighting to give an airy and generous feel to the main exhibition spaces. The addition of the Turner Contemporary finally allows Margate to leave its knotted handkerchief and ice cream image firmly behind.

14 St George Street and 50 New Bond Street
London W1

ERIC PARRY ARCHITECTS
CLIENT: SCOTTISH WIDOWS & KLEINWORT BENSON
STRUCTURAL ENGINEER: RAMBOLL UK
SERVICES ENGINEER: HILSON MORAN PARTNERSHIP
M & E ENGINEERS: CHAPMAN BATHURST
CONTRACTOR: LEND LEASE (BASE BUILD); MITIE (FIT OUT)
CONTRACT VALUE: £35.98 MILLION
DATE OF COMPLETION: MAY 2011
GROSS INTERNAL AREA: 11,284 SQ M
IMAGES: TIM SOAR

This project is considerably more complex than simply inserting two office buildings into a rich and varied urban context and involves the reworking of the retained fabric as well as new work of exceptional quality. The 14 St George Street office building has been developed behind a terrace on St George Street and replacing a demolished building on Maddox Street. The rhythm and scale of the St George Street terrace has been referenced with 'rooms' behind the façade based on the line of party walls and with profiled plaster ceilings instead of a more commercially usual soffit. 50 New Bond Street is more modest in scale, with a distinguished façade on which curved bay windows project between faience panels, contributing to the visual liveliness of the street.

Exhibition Road
Exhibition Road, South Kensington, London SW7

DIXON JONES

CLIENT: ROYAL BOROUGH OF KENSINGTON & CHELSEA
STRUCTURAL ENGINEERING: ARUP
CONTRACTOR: BALFOUR BEATTY
CONTRACT VALUE: £25 MILLION
DATE OF COMPLETION: DECEMBER 2011
IMAGES: PATRICK O'SULLIVAN
MIDLISTED FOR RIBA STIRLING PRIZE

Dixon Jones won the design competition to integrate vehicle and foot traffic and provide an attractive pedestrian environment without unduly compromising the road's role as a key transport link. Their proposal employed a grand diagonal pattern in the paving which acknowledges the scale and grandeur of the street. As a result of long consultation with disability groups, colour, texture and scale are utilised to inform users of the extent and margins of the four metre wide 'safe areas' with continuous strips of 'corduroy' paving and drainage grilles contrasting with the background grey and diagonal pink granite setts. Street clutter has been reduced to a minimum. This project serves as an important exemplar for what can be achieved in making cities more liveable.

Hackney Marshes Centre
South Marsh, Homerton Road, London E9

STANTON WILLIAMS

CLIENT: LONDON BOROUGH OF HACKNEY
STRUCTURAL ENGINEER: WEBB YATES
SERVICES ENGINEER: ZISMAN BOWYER & PARTNERS
CONTRACTOR: JOHN SISK & SON
CONTRACT VALUE: CONFIDENTIAL
DATE OF COMPLETION: NOVEMBER 2010
GROSS INTERNAL AREA: 3,060 SQ M
IMAGES: HUFTON + CROW
MIDLISTED FOR RIBA STIRLING PRIZE

Hackney Marshes is the home of amateur Sunday League football in London. The new Hackney Centre provides a 'community hub' comprising new changing rooms, a café and an education facility for players and the wider community. The restrained palette of rubble-filled gabions and corten steel makes reference to the historic uses of the site, while the building's simple, linear form creates a defining edge and gateway to the park. Despite the robust and relatively economic nature of these materials Stanton Williams's typically considered attention to composition and detailing give a feeling of elegance and refinement throughout. In response to the building's relatively isolated location, large sliding perforating corten screens 'lock down' the Centre at night, further enhancing its sculptural presence within the marsh landscape.

Henrietta Barnett School

Central Square, Hampstead Garden Suburb,
London NW11

HOPKINS ARCHITECTS

CLIENT: HENRIETTA BARNETT SCHOOL
STRUCTURAL ENGINEER: JANE WERNICK ASSOCIATES
CONTRACTOR: OSBORNE
CONTRACT VALUE: CONFIDENTIAL
DATE OF COMPLETION: FEBRUARY 2012
GROSS INTERNAL AREA: 1,132 SQ M
IMAGES: RICHARD BRINE

The original school was designed Lutyens and is listed Grade
II*. Any change of any kind was going to be controversial
and seventeen redevelopment schemes have previously
been rejected. Following intensive consultation the practice
drew up a masterplan for the whole campus stipulating much
smaller buildings with external circulation along colonnades
at two levels. Each new L-shaped wing extends directly from
the cross-axis of the Lutyens buildings. The buildings are
constructed with lime mortar brickwork and clay tiled roofs.
Outwardly the building is evidently designed to last, it is
robust and in that sense very sustainable. The interiors are
equally materially strong and well daylit. Hopkins Architects'
school buildings are a timely reminder of the value of carefully
designed educational environments.

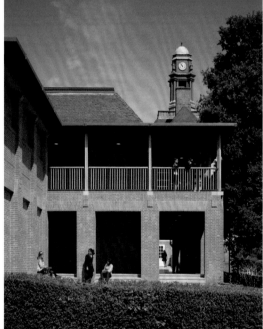

The Hurlingham Club Outdoor Pool
Ranelagh Gardens London SW6

DAVID MORLEY ARCHITECTS

CLIENT: THE HURLINGHAM CLUB
STRUCTURAL ENGINEER: SCOTT WHITE AND HOOKINS
SERVICES ENGINEER: HOARE LEA
CONTRACTOR: B&K BUILDING SERVICES
CONTRACT VALUE: CONFIDENTIAL
DATE OF COMPLETION: AUGUST 2011
GROSS INTERNAL AREA: 520 SQ M
IMAGES: JAROSŁAW WIECZORKIEWICZ

The Outdoor Pool was commissioned to replace a pool complex started 80 years ago, now dilapidated but still much loved by its members. The new changing room building is larger than the original and adopts an elongated tear shape; it reprises its predecessor with long horizontal proportions, blue painted clap-board walls with white doors and accessories such as the clock and life-saving rings. This reinterpretation of a traditional lido building is however given additional interest by the new roof which is made up of a series of elegant metal clad vaults which float at a constant height above clerestorey glazing. Hurlingham Outdoor Pool is a delightful complex reflecting the charm of a Lido in an exceptionally well-considered and executed whole.

Peabody Avenue, Pimlico
Peabody Avenue, London SW1

HAWORTH TOMPKINS

CLIENT: PEABODY
STRUCTURAL ENGINEER: PRICE & MYERS
CONTRACTOR: MANSELL CONSTRUCTION SERVICES
CONTRACT VALUE: £8.2 MILLION
DATE OF COMPLETION: APRIL 2011
IMAGES: PHILIP VILE

Peabody Avenue has been returned to its pre war-damaged
state with a building based on an understanding of the
characteristics of not only the form, texture and materiality
of the estate but also of the community which wished to
remain there. The five-storey high blocks, organised around
three vertical circulation cores, are built in warm, yellow
stock bricks with windows well set back in the manner of
the existing avenue's robust façades. To the rear, generous
balconies cantilever from the circulation walkway and
enliven the view from the railway and embankment. The new
building displays the strength, resilience and confidence
of the existing and is an exemplar of good housing and of
place-making.

Phase 1 Granary Complex: CSM Campus King's Cross

Granary Building, 1 Granary Square, London N1

STANTON WILLIAMS

CLIENT: ARGENT
STRUCTURAL ENGINEERS: SCOTT WILSON
CONTRACTOR: BAM CONSTRUCTION
CONTRACT VALUE: £145 MILLION
DATE OF COMPLETION: NOVEMBER 2011
GROSS INTERNAL AREA: 41,700 SQ M
IMAGES: HUFTON + CROW
MIDLISTED FOR RIBA STIRLING PRIZE

The success of the Granary Complex stems from the rich contrasts it achieves by juxtaposing and interweaving new and old. The 1851 Granary Building has been adapted as the college reception foyer, library and administrative offices. To the rear the Eastern and Western Transit Sheds frame a pair of new concrete studios, which are separated by a central north-south covered way redolent of a cathedral nave. Wide bridges link the studios across the 100m long space. A second transverse street establishes a public east-west route through the college. Stanton Williams have established a robust environment – home to 4,000 students and 1,000 staff – that does not depend on inert perfection but that can absorb the ebb and flow of students for many years to come.

Private House
London W6

HAYHURST AND CO.
IN COLLABORATION WITH LUCY CARM

CLIENT: PRIVATE
STRUCTURAL ENGINEER: WRIGHT CONSULTANCY GROUP
CONTRACTOR: REBUILD LONDON
CONTRACT VALUE: CONFIDENTIAL
DATE OF COMPLETION: OCTOBER 2011
GROSS INTERNAL AREA: 46 SQ M
IMAGES: KILLIAN O'SULLIVAN
WINNER OF RIBA LONDON SMALL PROJECT AWARD

Hairy House, named for the wildflower turf roof, is an extension to a Victorian terraced house, a mere 10 square metres larger than the previous footprint of a dilapidated lean-to, and in brief which required a new family kitchen, dining and play space. The simplicity of the brief was however accompanied by a desire to use the opportunities afforded by the angled and tapering geometry of the site playfully to challenge the existing house's Victorian order. Externally the solidity of the angular form of the building is expressed in precisely detailed rough-hewn slate which reinforces the notion that the extension is sunk into the ground. The result is a singular and very satisfying domestic environment which will long continue to intrigue and delight those who use it.

St Pancras Chambers
Euston Road, London NW1

RHWL ARCHITECTS
AND RICHARD GRIFFITHS ARCHITECTS

CLIENT: MANHATTAN LOFT CORPORATION
STRUCTURAL ENGINEER: ARUP
BUILDING ENGINEER: AECOM
CONTRACTOR: GALLIFORD TRY CONSTRUCTION SOUTH
CONTRACT VALUE: CONFIDENTIAL
DATE OF COMPLETION: NOVEMBER 2011
GROSS INTERNAL AREA: 32,249 SQ M
IMAGES: HUFTON + CROW
WINNER OF RIBA LONDON CLIENT OF THE YEAR AWARD
MIDLISTED FOR RIBA STIRLING PRIZE

In effect, this scheme completes the campaigning work led
by Sir John Betjeman and Nicholas Pevsner that saved Sir
George Gilbert Scott's building from demolition in the 1960s
and marked a watershed in the history of the conservation
movement. In its adapted form the internal spaces make
perfect sense. The architects internalised the original carriage
drop-off to create the hotel reception and a function room.
English Heritage insisted that the integration of en-suite
bathrooms should not be detrimental so they form diminutive
structures within the original room interiors. The mansard
roof has been adapted into an array of duplex of apartments.
Throughout decoration, lighting and carpeting have been
restored or reproduced. This painstaking work has returned a
true landmark to vibrant use.

St Paul's Church Hammersmith
Queen Caroline Street, London W6

RICHARD GRIFFITHS ARCHITECTS

CLIENT: ST PAUL'S CHURCH, HAMMERSMITH
STRUCTURAL ENGINEER: PRICE AND MYERS
SERVICES ENGINEER: MAX FORDHAM
CONTRACTOR: BRYEN & LANGLEY
CONTRACT VALUE: CONFIDENTIAL
DATE OF COMPLETION: OCTOBER 2011
GROSS INTERNAL AREA: 1,168 SQ M
IMAGES: WILL PRYCE

The new work carried out at the Grade 11* listed St Paul's Hammersmith has been premised on a profound understanding of historical precedents developed within a contemporary sensibility, resulting in a confident articulation of the new and a sympathetic reworking of the existing fabric. Its spiritual life revived by the arrival of a congregation from the evangelical Holy Trinity Brompton, it fell to RGA to revive and expand the fabric of the church. Having done the repairs, the architects then proposed a new church to the west of the existing one. Externally the building references its listed neighbour but it is not deferential. Internally an in-situ concrete frame is exposed throughout, while a flush glazed slot in the atrium provides light to the basement.

White Cube Bermondsey
144-152 Bermondsey Street, London SE1

CASPER MUELLER KNEER ARCHITECTS
CLIENT: WHITE CUBE
STRUCTURAL ENGINEER: ATELIER ONE
SERVICES ENGINEER: BOB COSTELLO ASSOCIATES
CONTRACTOR: LIFE BUILD SOLUTIONS
CONTRACT VALUE: CONFIDENTIAL
DATE OF COMPLETION: FEBRUARY 2012
GROSS INTERNAL AREA: 5,440 SQ M
IMAGES: PAUL RIDDLE

This is a brilliantly simple and appropriate use of a former industrial space in a newly vibrant area as a super cool gallery. The internal spaces are structurally and environmentally independent, formed to give the correct conditions for all possible displays. All walls, whether permanent or temporary, register as flat white planes, shadow gapped throughout. The floor is ubiquitous, immaculately finished, polished concrete. The ceiling over the circulation area comprises light tubes set in black mesh, while the Gallery lighting gives a shadowless, even quality for the displays. The splendid range of private viewing rooms are very private and intended to entice the viewer to buy. It is impossible to conceive of the project being better handled.

THE RIBA REGIONAL AWARDS

Awards have been presented in the majority of the nations and regions for many years, involving separate calls for entry, different eligibility, criteria, timetables and judging panels.

The RIBA's awards system was overhauled in 2012, so that architects enter one set of awards, where previously they were required to enter at national and regional level (see page 96 for RIBA Awards). Existing regional awards continue to use their local name, eg White Rose Awards in Yorkshire, and The Downland Prize in the south and south east of England. New awards were established, with local names, in the national and regions where no local awards previously existed.

All entries are first visited by an architect to see if they merit a visit from a full regional jury of three, consisting of an architect chair from outside the region, one from that region and a 'lay' juror, such as an engineer, client, artist or journalist. These juries agree RIBA Regional Awards, and a series of regional special awards (drawn from regional and RIBA Awards) for small projects, conservation, sustainability, best client and the building of the year. They also make strong recommendations to the national Awards Group on RIBA Awards. All these awards are presented in the RIBA regions.

THE JUDGES

As per the RIBA Awards (see page 96).

Cape Cove
Shore Road, Helensburgh

CAMERON WEBSTER ARCHITECTS

CLIENT: PRIVATE
CONTRACT VALUE: £300,000
DATE OF COMPLETION: 2012
IMAGE: DARPLE PHOTOGRAPHY

A spectacular site, right at the water's edge, with a view across Loch Long, the plan has been completely reconfigured to create a large and sunny entrance hall. The original kitchen and dining were moved upstairs and extended with full height frameless glazing. A simple palette of materials and colours was used. This home is designed to command superb seaward views. It rises from its natural rock foundations as an extraordinarily uncompromising and alluring work of modernity.

Corinthian Club
Glasgow

G1 GROUP

CLIENT: GI GROUP
CONTRACT VALUE: £4.5 MILLION
IMAGE: RENZO MAZZOLINI PHOTOGRAPHY

Phase 2 of this project stripped out the previously installed bar and restaurant fittings allowing contemporary architectural interventions including access stairs connecting the ornate 'Tellers Hall' and the vaulted brick basement. Rather than compete with existing architectural details, simple, clean materials such as frameless glazing and polished stainless steel were used to emphasise the historic significance of the building. The conversion has created a collection of bars, restaurants, a casino, a club and lettable conference suites of unrivalled opulence.

Fore Street
Glasgow

HYPOSTYLE ARCHITECTS

CLIENT: WHITEINCH + SCOTSTOUN HOUSING ASSOCIATION
CONTRACT VALUE: £1.5 MILLION
IMAGE: TOM MANLEY

The site sits within an existing Victorian tenement perimeter. The brief was to provide affordable housing to rent in a very tight, narrow backcourt site. A new build five-storey block of flats on Fore Street maintains the scale of the adjacent tenements. The backcourt area comprises a series of two-storey houses and cottage flats. These new homes are bright, welcoming and ingeniously woven into the existing fabric of the city, providing a useful model for the future.

Forth Valley College of Further and Higher Education, Alloa Campus

REIACH AND HALL ARCHITECTS

CLIENT: FORTH VALLEY COLLEGE OF FURTHER AND HIGHER EDUCATION
CONTRACT VALUE: £12.3 MILLION
IMAGE: DAVE MORRIS PHOTOGRAPHY

The new campus on a steeply sloping site is designed to encourage social interaction between learners and staff from different disciplines. The architectural diagram was driven by pragmatic issues such as the need for flat ground for workshops and service yard. Classroom accommodation embraces views to the Ochils to the north. The recent growth in buildings for all stages of education has generated some of Scotland's most powerfully expressive new structures. Set within a mature hilltop landscape this new college is both inviting and stimulating.

Grödians
Lerwick

RICHARD GIBSON ARCHITECTS
CLIENT: HJALTLAND HOUSING ASSOCIATION
CONTRACT VALUE: £4.5 MILLION
IMAGE: PHATSHEEP PHOTOGRAPHY

In a place where winters are prolonged and harsh, extensive planting and landscaping has been designed to bring shelter and reduce wind chill. A vibrant colour scheme maintains visual warmth. Natural finished timber is also used extensively in landscaping and the traffic calming measures offering a child-friendly environment. This is a careful yet engaging new addition to the Lerwick landscape, understated in form but highly appealing .The Scandinavian-inspired simple timber elevations are somehow entirely suited to this special setting at this seaward edge of Scotland.

Heathfield Primary School
Ayr

HOLMES MILLER
CLIENT: SOUTH AYRSHIRE COUNCIL
CONTRACT VALUE: £3.7 MILLION
IMAGE: ANDREW LEE

The redevelopment and extension of the existing school sought to respect original scale, remove the clutter to the rear and allow the extension to interlock with the old building. The building is composed of simple elements to deliver clean, crisp, elegant lines which ensure a contemporary architectural appearance, contrasting with, yet complementing, the original school building. Combining an established school with a very substantial new extension was a particular challenge which has been well met. This is an excellent environment for nurturing and stimulating young minds.

Heriot's Centre for Sport & Exercise
Edinburgh

LDN ARCHITECTS

CLIENT: GEORGE HERIOT'S TRUST
CONTRACT VALUE: CONFIDENTIAL
IMAGE: PAUL ZANRE

The need for large new volumes demanded careful handling
of the building's mass in this sensitive location to provide
state-of-the-art, contemporary accommodation. Studio space
is located on the first floor to allow a direct link between it
and the Sports Hall. Timber structure and lining gives the
main spaces a unique richness while a limited palette of
materials and colours add a feeling of warmth and welcome.
The external appearance of the building belies its innovative
use of timber technology.

House at Borreraig
Skye

DUALCHAS BUILDING DESIGN

CLIENT: PRIVATE
CONTRACT VALUE: £470,000
IMAGE: ANDREW LEE

The intention was to create a calm, contemplative space
for the client to escape the city. To keep the building low to
the skyline, it was broken up into three separate elements:
living, bedrooms and studio. Materials reflect the surrounding
landscape. The larch rainscreen gives a crisp external finish
and ensures that the building does not intrude upon its
natural setting. The same restraint and reliance on natural
materials, with a simple palette of Caithness stone and oak, is
evident in the uncluttered interiors.

Linlithgow Burgh Halls

MALCOLM FRASER ARCHITECTS
CLIENT: WEST LOTHIAN COUNCIL
CONTRACT VALUE: £3.2 MILLION
IMAGE: DAVE MORRIS

The Burgh Halls are of the greatest historic and social
significance, dating from 1668. They have been revamped
into community and visitor facilities – multi-use function halls,
tourist information, interpretation, café and education rooms.
The works opened the building up at its heart, with an airy,
light-filled stair. Crucially important to the town, this re-use
of a key historic building brings new life and vitality – an
inspiring dialogue with the building's history. Long neglected,
the Burgh Halls are now an asset.

Loch Leven Bird Hide
Fife

ICOSIS ARCHITECTS
CLIENT: RURAL ACCESS COMMITTEE FOR KINROSS-SHIRE
CONTRACT VALUE: £34,000
IMAGE: ICOSIS ARCHITECTS

This is a small crafted structure: part hide, part bridge and
part screening of an enclosed viewing platform overhanging
the loch. The open gaps between boards reduce wind
loading and restrict visual disruption for the birds. This is a
place to stop and enjoy the natural beauty of the loch. For
a very modest budget, this building cleverly addresses the
needs of human visitors yet its form is raw and elemental,
seeming to grow as an appropriate foil to the natural
environment in which it sits.

Model 'D' House
Insch

GOKAY DEVECI
CLIENT: SYLVAN STUART TIMBER ENGINEERS AND LOG CONSTRUCTION
CONTRACT VALUE: £140,000
IMAGE: STUART JOHNSTONE PHOTOGRAPHY

This is an alternative contemporary design utilising home-grown timber, using the architectural language of traditional north east agricultural buildings. Large windows in the south façade take advantage of the solar gain and maximise views. An external rain screen provides shading and privacy where required. Although its shape is relatively familiar, the external envelope of this new dwelling is anything but. This is a durable new approach to designing a one-off house and a model for affordable housing stock in the countryside.

Scotsman Steps
Edinburgh

MCGREGOR BOWES + HAWORTH TOMPKINS
WITH MARTIN CREED
CLIENT: FRUITMARKET GALLERY, CITY OF EDINBURGH COUNCIL,
EDINBURGH WORLD HERITAGE
CONTRACT VALUE: £500,000
IMAGE: GAUTIER DEBLONDE

The Scotsman Steps, built between 1899 and 1902, link the Old and New Towns of Edinburgh. Over time poor maintenance, bad lighting, vandalism and neglect had created a threatening environment. The steps were repaired and resurfaced as an artwork by Martin Creed with different and contrasting marbles from all over the world, each step and landing a different colour. Now the long climb is enlivened by the extraordinary variety of stones which form the new steps. The external structure, fully restored, is also revealed as something rich in delight.

Wester Coates House
Edinburgh

ZONE ARCHITECTS
CLIENT: PRIVATE
CONTRACT VALUE: CONFIDENTIAL
IMAGE: PAUL ZANRE

Wester Coates House is a new villa in a conservation area of
Edinburgh matching the scale and grandeur of its neighbours.
The stone cubic form of the house is split to allow light deep
into the stairwell at the centre of the plan. The south side of
the building opens out to embrace the private garden. This
new building utilises a simple palette of high quality natural
materials and a very restrained external form to embrace
interiors built to high specification and infused with light.

Dunmurry Presbyterian Church

HALL BLACK DOUGLAS ALISTAIR BECKETT
BARRY MCCANN
JOHN MURPHY CIAT
CLIENT: DUNMERRY PRESBYTERIAN CHURCH
STRUCTURAL ENGINEER: WYG CONSULTING ENGINEERS
SERVICES ENGINEER: CALDWELL CONSULTING
CONTRACTOR: FELIX O'HARE
IMAGE: HALL BLACK DOUGLAS

Hall Black Douglas was tasked with creating a building to
meet multiple needs: a clearly defined church sanctuary; open
spaces for informal meetings; a large hall for social functions;
and small meeting rooms. The result is a confident statement
of the engagement and relevance of the church for all
generations. At the same time, it subtly maintains references
and connections to the original 1860s, polychromatic brick
building across the way. It strikes that difficult balance
between reverence for shared memories and an open attitude
to the town and communities.

Elmwood Hall

CONSARC CONSERVATION

CLIENT: QUEEN'S UNIVERSITY BELFAST
CONTRACTOR: FELIX O'HARE
IMAGE: MARKETING AND CREATIVE SERVICES, QUEEN'S UNIVERSITY BELFAST

The restoration of the exterior of Elmwood Hall secures a
new life for this fine example of High Victorian architecture
as the University's projected new arts centre. The scheme
involved the repair of cracks, the insertion of new mouldings
and decorative detail; concrete repairs to the window tracery;
the re-pointing of stonework; the repair of metalwork repaired
and the re-gilding of the weather vane. This is a well-informed
and meticulous restoration of a prominent building that
restores its importance urbanistically and conveys its delight.

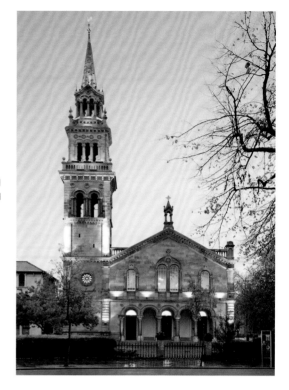

NORTH EAST

Institute of Transplantation
Freeman Road, High Heaton, Newcastle

RYDER ARCHITECTURE

CLIENT: NEWCASTLE UPON TYNE HOSPITALS NHS FOUNDATION TRUST
STRUCTURAL ENGINEER: ARUP
SERVICES ENGINEER: TGA CONSULTING ENGINEERS
CONTRACTOR: BAM CONSTRUCTION
CONTRACT VALUE: £25 MILLION
DATE OF COMPLETION: NOVEMBER 2011
GROSS INTERNAL AREA: 8,819 SQ M
IMAGE: KRISTEN MCCLUSKIE

This is a unique building type, the first in the UK to combine
an organ transplant facility with teaching. It is a functional, fit-
for-purpose building but the architects have challenged some
of the rules for hospital interior design that can make for
bland and unfriendly spaces. Externally they have responded
to the demand of the brief for a material palette of brick and
pre-patinated copper to match the adjacent buildings with
a well-proportioned and considered elevations that have
interest and respect their orientations.

Sleeperz Hotel
Westgate Road, Newcastle

CLASH ASSOCIATES

CLIENT: SLEEPERZ HOTELS
STRUCTURAL ENGINEER: CAPITA SYMONDS/WML CONSULTING
SERVICES ENGINEER: TANDY BUILDING SERVICES
CONTRACTOR: METNOR
CONTRACT VALUE: £7.5 MILLION
DATE OF COMPLETION: JANUARY 2012
GROSS INTERNAL AREA: 4,790 SQ M
IMAGE: SALLY ANN NORMAN

The Sleeperz Hotel concept is for hotels with small but stylish budget rooms built on the awkward left over spaces adjoining mainline railway termini. As an urban intervention it works extremely well with 'bookends' in Blaxter sandstone to match the neighbours. The Westgate Street elevation has a subtle curve and is highly glazed offering views down the street. The railway elevation, clad in zinc tiles, has angled projecting bay windows that direct views across Newcastle instead of over the car park below.

Theatre Royal
Grey Street, Newcastle Upon Tyne

SANSOME HALL ARCHITECTS

CLIENT: NEWCASTLE CITY COUNCIL
STRUCTURAL ENGINEER: CUNDALL JOHNSON
SERVICES ENGINEER: MAX FORDHAM
CONTRACTOR: SURGO CONSTRUCTION
CONTRACT VALUE: £4.096 MILLION
DATE OF COMPLETION: SEPTEMBER 2011
GROSS INTERNAL AREA: 2,500 SQ M
IMAGE: SALLY ANNE NORMAN
WINNER OF RIBA REGIONAL CONSERVATION AWARD

The redesign and conservation of the theatre, and particularly the multi-tiered auditorium, is extraordinarily consistent and seamless. The brief called for the sorting out of difficult access issues, restoring the original Frank Matcham rake to the upper tier and removing years of accretions that undermined the theatrical experience. A considerable amount of the interior finishes had to be re-invented since few records remain; where there was evidence the finishes were carefully researched and reinstated. The result is a theatre fit for the twenty-first century.

West Oak Farm
Broomley, Stocksfield, Northumberland

SPENCE AND DOWER

CLIENT: HALLYARDS DEVELOPMENTS
STRUCTURAL ENGINEER: GREENER WHITEHOUSE ASSOCIATES
CONTRACTOR: HALLYARDS DEVELOPMENTS
CONTRACT VALUE: CONFIDENTIAL
DATE OF COMPLETION: NOVEMBER 2011
GROSS INTERNAL AREA: 1,087 SQ M
IMAGE: HOLLY EVE WATSON

The scheme makes four dwellings out of an old farm and sets
new standards for the re-use of derelict agricultural buildings
in the region. Historic accretions to the farm buildings have
been stripped away and the new lightweight structures with
timber panelling and metal roofs have been well integrated.
The forms of the new buildings echo a modern industrial
aesthetic and are robustly detailed. The interiors make
the most of their south-facing aspect whether looking into
courtyards or onto open countryside.

Devonshire Road
Devonshire Road, Chorlton, Manchester

OLLIER SMURTHWAITE ARCHITECTS

CLIENT: PRIVATE CLIENT
STRUCTURAL ENGINEER: SHARPE TOPPING
CONTRACTOR: RBC (NORTHWEST)
CONTRACT VALUE: CONFIDENTIAL
DATE OF COMPLETION: OCTOBER 2011
GROSS INTERNAL AREA: 114 SQ M
IMAGE: MATT OLLIER
WINNER OF RIBA REGIONAL SMALL PROJECT AWARD

The rear extension adds a kitchen, dining and utility areas
and is full of light with a large frameless glazed window
overlooking the garden, and roof lights placed to reinforce
the kitchen space and the circulation route. The glazed units
wrap around the corner of the rear and side elevations so the
whole dissolves into the garden. Everything in the scheme has
been detailed with conviction. It reveals all the ingenuity and
delight that good architecture can bring to a small project.

The Moat House
Cheshire

BUTTRESS FULLER ALSOP WILLIAMS

CLIENT: PRIVATE
STRUCTURAL ENGINEER: ARJ ASSOCIATES
SERVICES ENGINEER: SILCOCK LEEDHAM
CONTRACTOR: IVY HOMES
CONTRACT VALUE: CONFIDENTIAL
DATE OF COMPLETION: OCTOBER 2010
GROSS INTERNAL AREA: 580 SQ M
IMAGE: ANTHONY REDMOND

This large family home more resembles a traditional farm.
Within the cluster of buildings is a garage, a pool house and
the main family home which is itself subdivided by a glazed
link which illuminates the internal circulation. The separate
buildings are connected at basement level to provide a single
dwelling. The quality of the detailing and the juxtaposition
of the buildings of different scale and footprint, succeed in
making a large scale family home into an intriguing cluster of
smaller buildings.

Richard Rose Morton Academy
Wigton Road, Carlisle

BDP

CLIENT: RICHARD ROSE MORTON ACADEMY/CUMBRIA COUNTY COUNCIL
STRUCTURAL ENGINEER: BDP
SERVICES ENGINEER: BDP
CONTRACTOR: KIER CONSTRUCTION
CONTRACT VALUE: £20.4 MILLION
DATE OF COMPLETION: SEPTEMBER 2011
GROSS INTERNAL AREA: 10,608 SQ M
IMAGE: DAVID BARBOUR
WINNER OF RIBA REGIONAL CLIENT OF THE YEAR AWARD

The design of this 1,150 pupil school underpins the teaching
methodology and allows for a significant level of flexibility,
with moving walls and interlocking spaces, exploring the
boundaries of how space is used to deliver and extend
learning. Instead of enclosed corridors, all circulation spaces
open to the central atrium, reinforcing the connection
between pupils and staff, and reducing bullying.
The exterior of the building has a robust brick plinth, with
vertical cedar staves above used to dissolve the overall mass
of the building.

Rigg Beck
Cumbria

KNOX BHAVAN

CLIENT: PRIVATE
STRUCTURAL ENGINEER: TWEDDELL & SLATER
SERVICES ENGINEER: MENDICK WARING
CONTRACTOR: COX & ALLEN
CONTRACT VALUE: CONFIDENTIAL
DATE OF COMPLETION: MAY 2011
GROSS INTERNAL AREA: 445 SQ M
IMAGE: CHARLES HOSEA PHOTOGRAPHY

This substantial house, in the Lake District National Park, is approached at an upper level, allowing its scale to be concealed within the landscape. Dry stone walls anchor the building to the land and a slate roof is punctuated by circular stone chimneys. On the side facing the river, the greater scale is reduced by an undulating timber-clad wall. The project is characterised by the commitment to craftsmanship and the use of found materials within a contemporary design.

Vaugh Steil
Bampton, Penrith

O'NEIL ASSOCIATES/O'NEIL AND PETRIE

CLIENT: PRIVATE
STRUCTURAL ENGINEER: GRASMERE STRUCTURAL ENGINEERS
CONTRACTOR: NIELSENS
CONTRACT VALUE: CONFIDENTIAL
DATE OF COMPLETION: JULY 2011
GROSS INTERNAL AREA: 376 SQ M
IMAGE: MATTHEW NICOL
WINNER OF RIBA REGIONAL CONSERVATION AWARD

There is an ever-increasing demand for houses in the Lake District so the issue of how to convert redundant farm buildings without impairing the character of the fells is crucial. Vaugh Steil is therefore a case study. The twin objectives of conservation and sustainability were revealed in the thoroughness with which materials were researched and tested. The project incorporates a wind turbine, solar thermal panels and photo-voltaics, coupled with a high performance, air-tight thermal and the use of high quality locally sourced materials with low embodied energy.

Ad++ House
Trentholme Drive, The Mount, York

COFFEY ARCHITECTS

CLIENT: PRIVATE
STRUCTURAL ENGINEER: ELLIOT WOOD
CONTRACTOR: MHD YORK
CONTRACT VALUE: CONFIDENTIAL
DATE OF COMPLETION: AUGUST 2011
GROSS INTERNAL AREA: 45 SQ M
IMAGE: TIM SOAR
WINNER OF RIBA REGIONAL SMALL PROJECT AWARD

This was a project of surprise and delight. The new extension makes complete sense of a house designed upside down due to its location on a site surrounded by a two-storey wall. The architect resisted tinkering with the existing house but developed a further aesthetic with a highly articulated structurally glazed addition which both belongs, and is of its own, dissolving the distinction between inside and outside. This is a scheme where ideas have been seamlessly integrated into the project to the joy of all.

Cliffe Hill Primary School
Stoney Lane, Halifax

AEDAS ARCHITECTS

CLIENT: CALDERDALE COUNCIL
STRUCTURAL ENGINEER: FURNESS PARTNERSHIP
SERVICES ENGINEER: WATERMAN GROUP
CONTRACTOR: WILLMOTT DIXON CONSTRUCTION
CONTRACT VALUE: £5 MILLION
DATE OF COMPLETION: MAY 2011
GROSS INTERNAL AREA: 2,185 SQ M
IMAGE: SIMON MILES

This project was an opportunity to commission a design-led educational building, hopefully pointing the way for further schools in the clients development programme. The use of the section on the sloping site was excellent. Spaces within the building were light and airy, the central courtyard was lively and well used, and each classroom on the ground floor had a simple and easy relationship with dedicated outside activity space. Thanks to thoughtful planning and execution, this building has been well received by the community it belongs to.

Horsefield House
Sheffield

PRUE CHILES ARCHITECTS

CLIENT: PRIVATE
STRUCTURAL ENGINEER: MARTIN EVANS ASSOCIATES
CONTRACTOR: JOHN SUNTER BUILDERS
CONTRACT VALUE: CONFIDENTIAL
DATE OF COMPLETION: OCTOBER 2011
GROSS INTERNAL AREA: 72 SQ M
IMAGE: PETER LATHEY

The commission was for a small half metre extension, however it became clear that much more was possible; a kitchen dining space with the kind of presence the original Victorian rooms had, and a fantastic courtyard garden bathed in sunlight. The result is an excellent example of how a modest extension can change the entire experience of a house, complenting and completing it, whilst providing a whole new set of possibilities. This is a lovely example of how a client's expectations can be expanded by working with an architect.

M&S Simply Foods
Eccleshall Road, Sheffield

LEWIS & HICKEY

CLIENT: MARKS & SPENCER
STRUCTURAL ENGINEER: WSP PROPERTY & DEVELOPMENT
SERVICES ENGINEER: SUSTAINABLE DESIGN SOLUTIONS
CONTRACTOR: WATES RETAIL
CONTRACT VALUE: £7.5 MILLION
DATE OF COMPLETION: APRIL 2011
GROSS INTERNAL AREA: 1,976 SQ M
IMAGE: FEARGAL O'CEALLAIGH

This supermarket takes a simple form and is built of second-hand bricks with signage painted onto the brickwork reminiscent of the old Sheffield grocer's stores.
As the M&S flagship green store, the building heats itself from the chilled food cabinets, re-used 98% of the material found on site and has a very thorough low-energy lighting and ventilating strategy. The architects have given something back to the street in a form that is a model other chains should learn from.

Beacon Heating
Capel Lawn

NIALL MAXWELL (JVC)
CLIENT: BEACON HEATING
CONTRACTOR: FIRTH CONSTRUCTION
CONTRACT VALUE: CONFIDENTIAL
DATE OF COMPLETION: AUGUST 2011
GROSS INTERNAL ARE: 95 SQ M
IMAGE: ROA

Small scale, often perfunctory buildings make up the fabric
of daily experience and to elevate something from the
everyday to something special is an achievement. This small
showroom for a wood energy appliance retailer is designed
to celebrate wood, both as a renewable energy source and a
construction material. It is an unexpected delight, beautifully
detailed, highly crafted and an eloquent demonstration of the
client's commitment to sustainability. It is also an exemplar for
industrial buildings in rural areas.

Carreg a Gwydr
Itton Common, Monmouthshire

HALL BEDNARCZYK
CLIENT: DR T COULSON
CONTRACTOR: MACCORMACK CONSTRUCTION
CONTRACT VALUE: £740,000
DATE OF COMPLETION: MAY 2011
GROSS INTERNAL AREA: 320 SQ M
IMAGE: MATT CANT

Carreg a Gwydr ('Stone and Glass') is in the Wye Valley Area
of Outstanding Natural Beauty. The design seeks to negotiate
the transition into open countryside by contrasting solidity
with transparency. The plan-form assumes an L-shape which
defines a living space from cellular study and utility area, and
upstairs, the master bedroom from three other bedrooms. A
naturally ventilated and top-lit double-height glazed entrance
area unites the two wings. The detailing is fine, inventive and
elegant and the building was conceived from the outset as a
low-energy dwelling.

Bushbury Hill Primary School
Old Fallings Lane, Wolverhampton

ARCHITYPE ARCHITECTS

CLIENT: WOLVERHAMPTON CITY COUNCIL
STRUCTURAL ENGINEER: PRICE & MYERS
SERVICES ENGINEER: E3 CONSULTING
CONTRACTOR: THOMAS VALE CONSTRUCTION
CONTRACT VALUE: CONFIDENTIAL
DATE OF COMPLETION: FEBRUARY 2012
GROSS INTERNAL AREA: 1, 900 SQ M
IMAGE: LEIGH SIMPSON
WINNER OF RIBA REGIONAL SUSTAINABILITY AWARD

With real mastery of scale and volume, a richness has emerged within this primary school from the separation of the two principal volumes, creating a central atrium. All credit to the design team that the Passivhaus accreditation was achieved and not at the expense of the user's experience. The orientation of the building enables it to benefit from appropriate solar control and passive gains. Care has been taken to ensure natural light reaches all classroom and corridor areas. Unfussy, with flawless detailing, this is a daringly ascetic building.

The Cube
Wharfside Street, Birmingham

MAKE

CLIENT: ARUNA PROJECT/BIRMINGHAM DEVELOPMENT COMPANY
STRUCTURAL ENGINEER: BURO HAPPOLD
SERVICES ENGINEER: HOARE LEA
CONTRACTOR: BUILDABILITY/ARUNA PROJECTS
CONTRACT VALUE: CONFIDENTIAL
DATE OF COMPLETION: AUGUST 2010
GROSS INTERNAL AREA: 42,000 SQ M
IMAGE: ZANDER OLSEN, MAKE

There is great sculptural invention here as well as a considered response to context on a grand scale. With meticulously investigated and detailed elevations, the 53 metre cube is topped with a coronet of public bars and restaurants. The architect's tenacity in refusing to compromise on the inclined structural glazing has to be applauded. Nowhere else in the city gives its residents such commanding views. This is development with generosity of spirit, and one must admire the patronage that has given a landmark to Birmingham.

The HUB, Coventry University
Jordan Well, Coventry

HAWKINS\BROWN

CLIENT: COVENTRY UNIVERSITY
STRUCTURAL ENGINEER: AKT II
SERVICES ENGINEER: MAX FORDHAM
CONTRACTOR: BAM CONSTRUCTION
CONTRACT VALUE: £19.5 MILLION
DATE OF COMPLETION: AUGUST 2011
GROSS INTERNAL AREA: 8,950 SQ M
IMAGE: TIM CROCKER

This is a pleasingly inventive and refreshingly visceral addition to the University's stock. By concentrating detail and visual effect in key areas, the architects have created surprise and intimacy within what is essentially a simple glass and concrete box. This is most obvious in the use of families of brightly finished furniture pods that house a welter of student activities including lounge areas, meeting pods, food offers and work areas. Overall a vibrant and popular building, and well-deserving winner of a regional award.

Queen Elizabeth Hospital Birmingham
Mindelsohn Way, Edgbaston, Birmingham

BUILDING DESIGN PARTNERSHIP

CLIENT: UNIVERSITY HOSPITALS BIRMINGHAM NHS FOUNDATION TRUST
STRUCTURAL ENGINEER: WHITE YOUNG GREEN
SERVICES ENGINEER: HULLEY & KIRKWOOD
CONTRACTOR: BALFOUR BEATTY AND HADEN YOUNG
CONTRACT VALUE: £582 MILLION
DATE OF COMPLETION: JUNE 2010
GROSS INTERNAL AREA: 137,000 SQ M
IMAGE: TIM SOAR
WINNER OF RIBA REGIONAL CLIENT OF THE YEAR AWARD

The handling of the scale of the project by the architects and the client's understanding of the benefits of the diagram are key elements to the success of this project. The careful handling of the way people move horizontally and vertically though the building prioritises patient privacy, while maximising efficiency of clinical care. Elliptical bedroom towers are an elegant solution to endless corridor syndrome, allowing the design to accommodate multiple ward configurations. This is a good example of an impressively controlled and well-considered building.

Severn Trent Water Regional Office
Shelton, Shrewsbury

GLENN HOWELLS ARCHITECTS

CLIENT: SEVERN TRENT WATER
STRUCTURAL ENGINEER: ARUP
SERVICES ENGINEER: ESC
CONTRACTOR: BAM CONSTRUCTION
CONTRACT VALUE: £7 MILLION
DATE OF COMPLETION: OCTOBER 2011
GROSS INTERNAL AREA: 2,686 SQ M
IMAGE: PAUL MCMULLIN

From a relatively complex brief, a simple, fit for purpose and extremely sustainable building has been created. Achieving a BREEAM Excellent standard, carbon emissions are four times lower than a typical office. By oversailing the cladding on a crisp stainless steel plinth out from the footings, the building appears to float above the ground. Setting the building in an integrated landscape of parking and rest space has created an interesting composition. This scheme stimulates, engages and delights occupants and visitors alike.

Wyre Forest Crematorium
Minster Road, Stourport on Severn

HOWL ASSOCIATES

CLIENT: DIGNITY/WYRE FOREST DISTRICT COUNCIL
STRUCTURAL ENGINEER: FAREBROTHER & PARTNERS
CONTRACTOR: HERBERT BAGGALEY CONSTRUCTION
CONTRACT VALUE: CONFIDENTIAL
DATE OF COMPLETION: OCTOBER 2011
GROSS INTERNAL AREA: 3,230 SQ M
IMAGE: HOWL ASSOCIATES

The degree of architectural ambition here is highly unusual, producing a distinctive, original response to a particularly testing challenge in form-as-function. A complex and ambitious composition has created spaces that have real serenity and gravitas. The slatted cedar soffits work well to unify the sequence of spaces both externally and internally. Great care has been taken with defining high-level clerestory light, particularly around the wedge-shaped chapel. With thought and consideration the architect leaves with us a building that stands scrutiny from all sides.

Catmose Campus
Catmose College, Huntsmans Drive, Oakham, Rutland

ELLIS MILLER

CLIENT: CATMOSE COLLEGE/RUTLAND COUNTY COUNCIL
STRUCTURAL ENGINEER: ELLIOTT WOOD
SERVICES ENGINEER: MAX FORDHAM
CONTRACTOR: GALLIFORD TRY
CONTRACT VALUE: £23 MILLION
DATE OF COMPLETION: FEBRUARY 2011
GROSS INTERNAL AREA: 311,434 SQ M
IMAGE: TIM SOAR

This new school for 900 students represents a clear departure from traditional school design – with an emphasis on flexible and adaptable daylit spaces. The design comprises of four independent 'modules' each of the same sized plan and separated from each other by promenades connecting to the landscape. One module is dedicated to the sports hall whilst the other three are teaching modules with large social spaces in the middle. Architect and client worked closely to develop a design which beautifully fulfills its ambitious brief.

Engineering & Science Learning Centre
University of Nottingham, University Park Campus, Nottingham

HOPKINS ARCHITECTS

CLIENT: UNIVERSITY OF NOTTINGHAM
STRUCTURAL ENGINEER: ARUP
SERVICES ENGINEER: ARUP
CONTRACTOR: MANSELL CONSTRUCTION SERVICES
CONTRACT VALUE: £7.5 MILLION
DATE OF COMPLETION: AUGUST 2011
GROSS INTERNAL AREA: 3,500 SQ M
IMAGE: MARTINE HAMILTON KNIGHT

The building sits at the heart of the Basil Spence campus and incorporates flexible teaching spaces, IT facilities, a social space and café, and a lecture theatre. The new building is a half-elliptical plan 'plugged' on to the parallel linear existing building and set in a garden court. A curved rain-screen wraps itself over the roof of the building, accentuating the free-standing nature of the new form. It is elegant, well-proportioned and beautifully considered and crafted – and makes an extremely positive contribution to the surrounding context.

Maggie's Nottingham
Nottingham City Hospital Campus,
Hucknall Road, Nottingham

CZWG

CLIENT: MAGGIE'S
STRUCTURAL ENGINEER: AKT II
SERVICES ENGINEER: KJ TAIT ENGINEERS
CONTRACTOR: BOWMER & KIRKLAND BUILDING SERVICES
CONTRACT VALUE: CONFIDENTIAL
DATE OF COMPLETION: NOVEMBER 2011
GROSS INTERNAL AREA: 360 SQ M
IMAGE: MARTINE HAMILTON KNIGHT

This alternative environment to hospital, where cancer
patients can learn more about their illness, is set on a wooded
site and entered via a footbridge. The kitchen/dining space –
crucial to the sense of welcoming intimacy – is located at the
centre of a square plan with smaller living and consultation
rooms wrapping around it. Externally the square plan is
concealed by the interlocking decorative 'hoops' with tile
inlay and protruding but sheltered balconies. The form is
intended to be both eye-catching and fun.

Uppingham School Sports Centre
Uppingham, Rutland

ORMS ARCHITECTURE DESIGN

CLIENT: UPPINGHAM SCHOOL
STRUCTURAL ENGINEER: BROOKBANKS CONSULTING
SERVICES ENGINEER: RAMBOLL UK
CONTRACTOR: BOWMER & KIRKLAND
CONTRACT VALUE: £11.5 MILLION
DATE OF COMPLETION: AUGUST 2010
GROSS INTERNAL AREA: 4,409 SQ M
IMAGE: ED HILL

The new sports centre for Uppingham School includes a 25
metre pool, a fitness studio, squash courts and gymnasium.
The building has a dual role in both serving the school and
the community. The potential long term income stream meant
the client could allow the design to be more ambitious.
ORMS developed a simple clear strategy for the site, entailing
a raised grass escarpment overlooking the rugby pitches.
The building was well planned, well considered and well
executed.

Victoria Leisure Centre
Gedling Street, Nottingham

LEVITATE

CLIENT: NOTTINGHAM CITY COUNCIL
STRUCTURAL ENGINEER: FURNESS PARTNERSHIP
CONTRACTOR: CARILLION/INSPIRED SPACES
CONTRACT VALUE: CONFIDENTIAL
DATE OF COMPLETION: JANUARY 2012
GROSS INTERNAL AREA: 3,100 SQ M
IMAGE: MARTINE HAMILTON KNIGHT

The Victoria Leisure Centre is a new 3,000 square metre public facility built around a Victorian building. It incorporates swimming pools, gym and fitness studios, a café and foyer. Externally the building offers a large civic frontage to the existing main public square at a scale and in an architectural language appropriate to its civic status. Sitting on a raised plinth, the pool has a large north-lit timber roof structure beautifully finessed with a series of delicate timber diagonal baffles. This is a lovely project.

Emmanuel College Library
St Andrews Street, Cambridge

KILBURN NIGHTINGALE ARCHITECTS

CLIENT: EMMANUEL COLLEGE
STRUCTURAL ENGINEER: PRICE AND MYERS
SERVICES ENGINEER: RAMBOLL
CONTRACTOR: KILLBY AND GRAYFORD
CONTRACT VALUE: £5.0 MILLION
DATE OF COMPLETION: OCTOBER 2011
GROSS INTERNAL AREA: 2,200 SQ M
IMAGE: NICK KANE

Turning a 1970s concrete frame archive store into a library that is suited to exploring the relationships between books, fellow students, and with the act of reading itself, whilst improving the environmental performance of the building, was no easy task. A diverse range of spaces for reading and studying has been created in what is now an extension to the existing Edwardian library. The lightweight timber structure housing individual reading carrels also houses lighting and trickle ventilation.

Lee Valley White Water Centre
Station Road, Waltham Cross, Herts

FAULKNER BROWNS ARCHITECTS
CLIENT: LEE VALLEY REGIONAL PARK AUTHORITY
STRUCTURAL ENGINEER: CUNDALL
SERVICES ENGINEER: CUNDALL
CONTRACTOR: GALLIFORD TRY (MORRISON)
CONTRACT VALUE: £25 MILLION
DATE OF COMPLETION: OCTOBER 2010
GROSS INTERNAL AREA: 1,950 SQ M
IMAGE: PHILIP VILE

The building is set in an artificial landscape designed to create the rapidly moving water needed by those training and participating in the canoe events in the 2012 Olympic Games. It acts as both a sign and a hide in the landscape. The landscape's layering of views, heights and planting are key to the integration of water engineering and architecture, adding beauty to physical delight. In Legacy mode, maturing woodland will create a natural water park enjoyed by surrounding communities and visitors alike.

Private House
Madingley Road, Cambridge

MOLE ARCHITECTS
CLIENT: IAN AND SUE COLLINS
STRUCTURAL ENGINEER: RAMBOLL
SERVICES ENGINEER: RAMBOLL
CONTRACTOR: CAMBRIDGE BUILDING COMPANY
CONTRACT VALUE: £680,000
DATE OF COMPLETION: JULY 2010
GROSS INTERNAL AREA: 255 SQ M
IMAGE: DAVID BUTLER
WINNER OF RIBA EAST SUSTAINABILITY AWARD

On a busy road, a sequence of single-storeyed, sun-filled rooms off south and west facing corridors encircles a garden oasis. Each room has a strong relationship with the garden, the sky and the trees. The sequence culminates in a tall living space, looking back at the garden and its gatehouse. The energy performance is above the Passivhaus standard, testament that low-technology and excellence in spatial design, rather than the use of heavy mechanical systems, can achieve a higher standard of sustainable architecture.

Private House
Feering, Essex

HUDSON ARCHITECTS

CLIENT: BEN COODE-ADAMS
STRUCTURAL ENGINEER: THE MORTON PARTNERSHIP
CONTRACTOR: NS RESTORATIONS
CONTRACT VALUE: CONFIDENTIAL
DATE OF COMPLETION: NOVEMBER 2011
GROSS INTERNAL AREA: 525 SQ M
IMAGE: JAMES BRITTAIN
WINNER OF RIBA EAST CONSERVATION AWARD

Where others might have given up on this barn conversion, the architects have thought creatively to overcome local authority conservation rules. Large roof-lights are concealed under a plane of expanded steel mesh, maintaining the pure agricultural appearance that the planners had wanted but allowing light into the barn. From a distance the roof forms a sculptural monolithic mass that unfolds on approach into a charming complex of agricultural buildings from different eras. Inside spaces are filled with numerous materials found, reclaimed and reused.

Royal Opera House
Production Workshop
Purfleet Bypass, Purfleet

NICHOLAS HARE ARCHITECTS

CLIENT: THE ROYAL OPERA HOUSE
STRUCTURAL ENGINEER: ARUP
SERVICES ENGINEER: ARUP
CONTRACTOR: MCLAREN
CONTRACT VALUE: £6.1 MILLION
DATE OF COMPLETION: NOVEMBER 2011
GROSS INTERNAL AREA: 4,300 SQ M
IMAGE: HUFTON + CROW

The workshop is dedicated to light and to the craft of making. The vaulted structure creates a grand assembly space, serviced and viewed from the surrounding metal and timber workshops and office spaces. The comings and goings of the craftspeople and sets, together with the size of the entrances, suggest that this is a building that will provoke great local interest and even have an educational purpose. This is a public building as much as it is a private one.

Stable Acre
Duck Row, Haveringland, Norfolk

DAVID KOHN ARCHITECTS

CLIENT: PRIVATE
STRUCTURAL ENGINEER: ALAN BAXTER + ASSOCIATES
SERVICES ENGINEER: CONSERVATION ENGINEERING/MAX FORDHAM
CONTRACTOR: H SMITH & SONS
CONTRACT VALUE: CONFIDENTIAL
DATE OF COMPLETION: MARCH 2010
GROSS INTERNAL AREA: 234 SQ M
IMAGE: WILL PRYCE

Monastic simplicity in plan and finishes characterise this
renovation of a nineteenth-century stable block. The rooms
form a simple line of spaces with double-glazed steel windows
in the living and dining areas opening up completely, baring
the house to nature. Due to its compactness of the plan and
continuous south-facing double-glazed facades, underfloor
heating and a single wood-burning stove are sufficient to
heat the house. White emulsion finished oak panels highlight
their rough-sawn texture whilst creating the ethereal and
puritanical ambience.

Colston's Girls' School
Cheltenham Road, Bristol

WALTERS AND COHEN

CLIENT: PRIVATE
STRUCTURAL ENGINEER: SKANSKA TECHNOLOGY
SERVICES ENGINEER: OVE ARUP & PARTNERS
CONTRACTOR: SKANSKA CONSTRUCTION
CONTRACT VALUE: CONFIDENTIAL
DATE OF COMPLETION: SEPTEMBER 2011
GROSS INTERNAL AREA: 8,343 SQ M
IMAGE: DENNIS GILBERT

By intelligently re-organising spaces and routes, this project
deals with many of the difficulties to do with the site and
the programme. The confident new building cleverly wraps
around existing buildings creating a coherent collection of
spaces. A new theatre opening onto the street, encourages
public access; the brick façade reflects patterns and tones
from the original building; recycled teak lab benches are
used in the public spaces. This is successful, unpretentious
architecture, which has restored a school's sense of its status
in the local community.

King's College Library
South Road, Taunton, Somerset

MITCHELL TAYLOR WORKSHOP

CLIENT: KINGS COLLEGE
STRUCTURAL ENGINEER: HYDROCK STRUCTURES 1
SERVICES ENGINEER: BURO HAPPOLD
CONTRACTOR: RG SPILLER
CONTRACT VALUE: £1.42 MILLION
DATE OF COMPLETION: JUNE 2011
GROSS INTERNAL AREA: 650 SQ M
IMAGE: PETER COOK

This new library is a thoughtful insertion into a restricted site alongside existing Grade II listed buildings. With local stone quarries exhausted, the architects developed a bespoke brick, its colour and texture harmonising with the existing stone. 'Witches hat' north lights animate the principal façade, bringing in light and natural ventilation, their bold expression, together with the crafted brickwork, giving the building its identity. The library is a successful, light, airy space, which has delighted the client and is enjoyed by all the pupils.

The Seagull & The Windbreak
Undercliffe Drive, Boscombe, Dorset

A:B:I:R ARCHITECTS AND PETER FRANCIS LEWIS

CLIENT: BOURNEMOUTH BOROUGH COUNCIL
STRUCTURAL ENGINEER: INGS ENGINEERING
CONTRACTOR: PUSH STUDIOS
CONTRACT VALUE: £100,000
DATE OF COMPLETION: AUGUST 2011
GROSS INTERNAL AREA: 35 SQ M
IMAGE: RICHARD ROWLAND

As the UK's first beach huts designed specifically for people with disabilities, this project represents a creative response to a demanding brief. Considered organisation of space allows much flexibility. The 'Seagull', the wing form of the roof, is a simple, distinctive device unifying the four huts. The 'Windbreak', the billowing coloured banding, enforces this identity providing visual messaging for the partially sighted. This is an exciting modest project, where both user and client see its impact acting as a catalyst for wider design improvements along the seafront.

Sherborne Music School
Abbey Road, Sherbourne, Dorset

ORMS ARCHITECTURE DESIGN

CLIENT: SHERBORNE SCHOOL
STRUCTURAL ENGINEER: TALL STRUCTURES
SERVICES ENGINEER: ERNEST GRIFFITHS & SONS
CONTRACTOR: KEN BIGGS CONTRACTORS
CONTRACT VALUE: £2.4 MILLION
DATE OF COMPLETION: JULY 2010
GROSS INTERNAL AREA: 1,074 SQ M
IMAGE: KILLIAN O'SULLIVAN

Sitting comfortably in a mature garden setting, this project takes full advantage of the views. A simple diagram organises the accommodation around a central roof-lit atrium. The new music rooms delight with their connection to the surrounding trees as well as meeting demanding acoustic requirements. The façades have been carefully detailed with timber cladding above a stone base. The client was truly delighted with the outcome and is certain this school offers the perfect environment to nurture the creative talents of its students.

Tyntesfield House
– repair and refurbishment
Wraxall, Somerset

RODNEY MELVILLE & PARTNERS

CLIENT: THE NATIONAL TRUST
STRUCTURAL ENGINEER: MANN WILLIAMS
SERVICES ENGINEER: GIFFORD (NOW RAMBOLL)
CONTRACTOR: C S WILLIAMS
CONTRACT VALUE: CONFIDENTIAL
DATE OF COMPLETION: DECEMBER 2010
GROSS INTERNAL AREA: 3,510 SQ M
IMAGE: MATT SWEETING PHOTOGRAPHY
WINNER OF RIBA REGIONAL CONSERVATION AWARD

Discreet architectural surgery allowed Tyntesfield to be captured at its final inhabited hour. Essential new services, systems and a lift have been cleverly integrating into the Grade I listed fabric, allowing it to work as a twenty-first century tourist attraction. Architectural ingenuity throughout the conservation process was needed to meet the need for continuous public access, whilst accommodating the roosting patterns of colonies of bats. This is a hugely impressive conservation project in terms of both quality and execution.

Douai Abbey
Upper Woolhampton, Reading, Berkshire

DAVID RICHMOND AND PARTNERS

CLIENT: FATHER OLIVER HOLT
STRUCTURAL ENGINEER: PRICE AND MYERS
CONTRACTOR: FELTHAM CONSTRUCTION
CONTRACT VALUE: £3.8 MILLION
DATE OF COMPLETION: JANUARY 2010
GROSS INTERNAL AREA: 2,465 SQ M
IMAGE: DAVID RICHMOND

The architects were asked to reconfigure and refurbish what had been an Abbey Church and latterly a school, creating a retreat centre and adding new accessible accommodation for both monks and their guests. They responded with a new wing which means the guests do not come into contact with the monks. This is a modest, even humble piece of work, but the quality of the architecture shines through. The library is a place where you want to sit and read books forever.

Egypt Galleries, Ashmolean Museum
Oxford

RICK MATHER ARCHITECTS

CLIENT: ASHMOLEAN MUSEUM
STRUCTURAL ENGINEER: PRICE & MYERS
SERVICES ENGINEER: HOARE LEA
CONTRACTOR: BEARD CONSTRUCTION
CONTRACT VALUE: CONFIDENTIAL
DATE OF COMPLETION: NOVEMBER 2011
GROSS INTERNAL AREA: 1,016 SQ M
IMAGE: ANDY MATTHEW, RICK MATHER ARCHITECTS

This is a modest scheme for a stunning collection. The architects were appointed in 1999 to develop a masterplan for the Ashmolean, to provide more space and twenty-first century facilities for its collections. Phase One was shortlisted for the Stirling prize in 2010. Phase Two of the masterplan involved the extension and renovation of the Egypt Galleries. The work, which is done with these architects' always meticulous attention to detail, completes the circular route, so the Egyptian story is told for the first time in sequence.

Endeavour Primary School
East Anton Farm Road, Andover, Hampshire

HAMPSHIRE COUNTY COUNCIL

CLIENT: HAMPSHIRE COUNTY COUNCIL
STRUCTURAL ENGINEER: RAMBOLL
SERVICES ENGINEER: WSP BUILDINGS
CONTRACTOR: MANSELL CONSTRUCTION SERVICES
CONTRACT VALUE: £6.346 MILLION
DATE OF COMPLETION: NOVEMBER 2011
GROSS INTERNAL AREA: 2,320 SQ M
IMAGE: TOM HEATHERINGTON

This is a new primary school for 420 pupils delivered in the great tradition of Hampshire Schools, in which the children's needs are primary to the design. The brief called for flexible accommodation that can adapt to changing learning styles in the future. The design involves simple dual-pitched roofed buildings around a central courtyard with the main school hall on the street front, all linked by flat roofed, glazed cloisters. The building forms allow each class a two metre deep covered external space for outdoor learning.

Forest Park Primary School
Ringwood Road, Totton, Southampton, Hampshire

HAMPSHIRE COUNTY COUNCIL

CLIENT: HAMPSHIRE COUNTY COUNCIL, CHILDREN'S SERVICES
STRUCTURAL ENGINEER: WSP GROUP
SERVICES ENGINEER: HAMSPHIRE COUNTY COUNCIL, PROPERTY SERVICES
CONTRACTOR: MORGAN SINDALL
CONTRACT VALUE: £8.9 MILLION
DATE OF COMPLETION: JULY 2011
GROSS INTERNAL AREA: 3,025 SQ M
IMAGE: NIGEL BAKER

This Hampshire school, on the edge of the New Forest National Park, is for children with complex learning difficulties. In addition to the nine classrooms, the facilities include a nursery, hydrotherapy pool, multi-sensory room, a soft play area, and therapy rooms. But such a school cannot just be about facilities. It must engender a sense of well-being, even pride among pupils and staff. The architects have created an extraordinary place in which pupils feel special only in the best sense of the word.

Fort Nelson
Portsdown Hill Road, Fareham, Hampshire

PRINGLE RICHARDS SHARRATT ARCHITECTS

CLIENT: ROYAL ARMOURIES
STRUCTURAL ENGINEER: RAMBOLL
SERVICES ENGINEER: RAMBOLL
CONTRACTOR: MANSELL
CONTRACT VALUE: £3.8 MILLION
DATE OF COMPLETION: AUGUST 2011
GROSS INTERNAL AREA: 3,800 SQ
IMAGE: EDMUND SUMNER
WINNER OF RIBA REGIONAL CONSERVATION AWARD

Fort Nelson is essentially a glorified but glorious lean-to against the massive fortifications that make up this Victorian gun fort overlooking Portsmouth Harbour. Beautifully designed by Pringle Richards Sharratt (out of Hopkins), the timber structure is almost an exhibit in itself. But there is steel enough in the exhibits: this is home to the Royal Armouries' national collection of historic artillery. The design involved turning the museum on its head by creating an entrance across an existing draw bridge.

Long House
Winchester, Hampshire

DAN BRILL ARCHITECTS

CLIENT: PRIVATE
STRUCTURAL ENGINEER: HEYNE TILLET STEEL
CONTRACTOR: ROGER WARD
CONTRACT VALUE: £295,000
DATE OF COMPLETION: OCTOBER 2011
GROSS INTERNAL AREA: 210 SQ M
IMAGE: EDMUND SUMNER

Once again the perversity of planners has led to a small triumph of architecture. Planning required the retention of the old house and that the visual prominence of the development should be minimised. The old house has been gutted, providing a open-plan living in a double-height volume. A lovely stair can be read through obscured glass. Bedrooms are in a new single-storey wing at the rear. This is a fine example of making a silk purse from a sow's ear.

Old San Juan
Windsor Road, Gerrards Cross, Bucks

CORRIGAN + SOUNDY + KILAIDITI ARCHITECTS

CLIENT: PRIVATE
STRUCTURAL ENGINEER: IAN BIRD ASSOCIATES
CONTRACTOR: WALKER EMBURY
CONTRACT VALUE: £1.1 MILLION
DATE OF COMPLETION: NOVEMBER 2011
GROSS INTERNAL AREA: 550 SQ M
IMAGE: CATHERINE WILSON

This art deco house, originally commissioned by the Chairman of Cunard, was completed haphazardly and not in the spirit of the original. It was also in a very bad condition. The challenge was to reorganise and extend the house to create open plan useable spaces, and allow light to infiltrate all the rooms. This has been achieved by carefully considering every aspect of the design: from the geometrical form of the rear extension, down to the bespoke Deco detailing of the door handles.

Private House
Sonning

GREGORY PHILLIPS ARCHITECTS

CLIENT: PRIVATE
STRUCTURAL ENGINEER: RAMBOLL
SERVICES ENGINEER: MENDICK WARING
CONTRACTOR: KINGERLEE
CONTRACT VALUE: CONFIDENTIAL
DATE OF COMPLETION: JANUARY 2011
GROSS INTERNAL AREA: 850 SQ M
IMAGE: DARREN CHUNG

The modernist country house has become a significant building type of the early twenty-first century: concrete framed, using white render and stainless steel and highly glazed (but efficiently so). This project ticks all these boxes and more and gives the clients all they asked for and more. But it adds a very special flint-walled inner courtyard which is flanked by galleried corridors lined with timber and floored with stone. It admires itself in the reflecting pool across which you enter, rightly so.

Pond Cottage
Buckinghamshire

CHRIS BANNISTER AND BARBARA DUNSIRE

CLIENT: PRIVATE
STRUCTURAL ENGINEER: TAPSELL WADE & PARTNERS
CONTRACTOR: N & G GRAY & SONS
CONTRACT VALUE: CONFIDENTIAL
DATE OF COMPLETION: FEBRUARY 2011
GROSS INTERNAL AREA: 49 SQ M
IMAGE: CHRIS BANNISTER
REGIONAL SMALL PROJECT AWARD WINNER

Pond Cottage was once three cottages knocked together and modified over time. The exquisite new two-storey extension, which projects beyond the gable end of the existing house and contains a new garden room, a hallway and a master bedroom with en-suite, respects the local vernacular but clearly distinguishes the new construction from the old. A new handmade brick that complements the mix of bricks used before has been used both internally and externally in the new extension.

Pooley House
Hayling Island

JOHN PARDEY ARCHITECTS

CLIENT: JONATHAN POOLEY + DAWN REID
STRUCTURAL ENGINEER: RAMBOLL UK
CONTRACTOR: ANDREWS BUILDING
CONTRACT VALUE: £455,000
DATE OF COMPLETION: JULY 2010
GROSS INTERNAL AREA: 230 SQ M
IMAGE: JAMES MORRIS

The clients wanted a house to suit their outdoor lifestyle. The result caters equally well for wetsuits and al fresco dining. A masonry base supports a light, transversely arranged red cedar clad box that cantilevers over each side of the base. The staircase which slides up the outside of the building is enclosed with frameless glazing to act as a lantern. The energy strategy involves a highly insulated envelope, an air source heat pump producing underfloor heating and a wood burning stove.

Brighton Aldridge Community Academy
Lewes Road, Brighton

FEILDEN CLEGG BRADLEY STUDIOS

CLIENT: BRIGHTON AND HOVE CITY COUNCIL
STRUCTURAL ENGINEER: WSP BUILDINGS
CONTRACTOR: KIER SOUTHERN
CONTRACT VALUE: £22 MILLION
DATE OF COMPLETION: SEPTEMBER 2011
GROSS INTERNAL AREA: 11,375 SQ M
IMAGE: RICHARD CHIVERS
WINNER OF RIBA REGIONAL SUSTAINABILITY AWARD (SOUTH EAST)

This new academy, whose specialisms are Entrepreneurship and Sport, lies on the edge of the South Downs and has been designed as part of the landscape of the South Downs. The palette of materials is drawn from this landscape: flint, chalk and Anthracite bricks. The first floor has a system of full-height flush glazing creating a seamless smooth surface that contrasts with the textured ground floor. To reflect light into teaching spaces, a chalky white brick is used for the external wall.

G-Live Performing Arts Centre
London Road, Guildford, Surrey

AUSTIN-SMITH:LORD

CLIENT: GUILDFORD BOROUGH COUNCIL
STRUCTURAL ENGINEER: URS/SCOTT WILSON
SERVICES ENGINEER: GRONTMIJ
CONTRACTOR: WILMOTT DIXON CONSTRUCTION
CONTRACT VALUE: £21.5 MILLION
DATE OF COMPLETION: JULY 2011
GROSS INTERNAL AREA: 5,900 SQ M
IMAGE: ANDY MATTHEWS

This replacement for the old Guildford Civic Hall occupies a steeply sloping site and acts as an 'anchor' to the upper end of Guildford High Street. A diagonal public route passes the café, dips under the theatre auditorium, towards the studio theatre and park, encouraging the varied use of the foyer spaces throughout the day. The venue provides a performance venue for everything from classical music to rock, from comedy to ice shows, conferencing to banqueting – as well as a home for the Guildford Philharmonic Orchestra.

Maidstone Museum East Wing
St. Faith's Street, Maidstone, Kent

HUGH BROUGHTON ARCHITECTS

CLIENT: MAIDSTONE BOROUGH COUNCIL
STRUCTURAL ENGINEER: AECOM
SERVICES ENGINEER: AECOM
CONTRACTOR: MORGAN SINDALL
CONTRACT VALUE: £3 MILLION
DATE OF COMPLETION: OCTOBER 2011
GROSS INTERNAL AREA: 1,150 SQ M
IMAGE: HUFTON + CROW

Copper-clad diamond-patterned walls in the centre of Maidstone – whatever next? Grade II listed and dating back to 1561, the Museum was in terminal decline and in danger of closure. With thirteen changes in level, it did not comply with any current regulations. The client and architects have tackled all these problems with enthusiasm and verve. The new 'gold-clad' wings have provided substantial additional exhibition space and a 'window on the park', advertising the museum to passers-by in the park.

The Marlowe Theatre
The Friars, Canterbury, Kent

KEITH WILLIAMS ARCHITECTS

CLIENT: CANTERBURY CITY COUNCIL
STRUCTURAL ENGINEER: BURO HAPPOLD
SERVICES ENGINEER: MAX FORDHAM
THEATRE CONSULTANTS: CHARCOALBLUE
CONTRACTOR: ISG JACKSON
CONTRACT VALUE: £17.95 MILLION
DATE OF COMPLETION: SEPTEMBER 2011
GROSS INTERNAL AREA: 4,850 SQ M
IMAGE: HELENE BINET

The trick was to fit the inevitable mass of a theatre into the maze of Grade I listed buildings that makes up Canterbury's UNESCO World Heritage Site. The architects have achieved the near impossible with a white stone colonnade that wraps the foyer spaces and unified the composition. A sloping granite forecourt leads into the foyer and the 1,194 seat main auditorium. The flytower, second only in height to Cathedral tower, is clad in stainless steel mesh and lights up at night. Truly a landmark building.

Private House
West Sussex

GUY STANSFELD ARCHITECTS

CLIENT: PRIVATE
STRUCTURAL ENGINEER: PETER HYATT ASSOCIATES
SERVICES ENGINEER: BUILDING SERVICES DESIGN PARTNERSHIP
CONTRACTOR: RAI DEVELOPMENTS
CONTRACT VALUE: CONFIDENTIAL
DATE OF COMPLETION: FEBRUARY 2012
GROSS INTERNAL AREA: 800 SQ M
IMAGE: NICK KANE

This detached house overlooking the beach is remarkable
for the contrast between its rugged all-flint exterior and the
warmth of the interior. By excavating over 2 metres a guest
flat, garages and swimming pool have been incorporated at
lower-ground level. Rich timber interior linings are juxtaposed
with exposed concrete ceilings and untreated in situ cast
columns. The overall effect is to give a high degree of comfort
whilst reminding the occupants of the unforgiving nature of
the coastal climate outside. This is a real home.

Rocksalt Restaurant
Fishmarket, Folkestone, Kent

GUY HOLLAWAY ARCHITECTS

CLIENT: PRIVATE
STRUCTURAL ENGINEER: CAMPBELL REITH
SERVICES ENGINEER: MLM
CONTRACTOR: CARDY
CONTRACT VALUE: CONFIDENTIAL
DATE OF COMPLETION: JUNE 2011
GROSS INTERNAL AREA: 481 SQ M
IMAGE: PAUL FREEMAN

This new contemporary destination restaurant is a part of
Terry Farrell's Folkstone masterplan and forms the focal point
of the 2011 Folkestone Triennial, which entailed a strict
eighteen-month programme. Three curved walls are clad in
shot-blasted black larch; a slate plinth raises the building;
large glass sliding doors allow uninterrupted panoramic views
of the harbour; a cantilevered balcony, with glass balustrade
and curved zinc soffit, creates an extension of the internal
dining area.

Simon Smith Building
Eastern Road, Brighton, East Sussex

ALLIES & MORRISON

CLIENT: BRIGHTON COLLEGE
STRUCTURAL ENGINEER: FLUID STRUCTURES
SERVICES ENGINEER: FOSTER AND PARTNERS
CONTRACTOR: PRIMUS BUILD
CONTRACT VALUE: CONFIDENTIAL
DATE OF COMPLETION: JANUARY 2012
GROSS INTERNAL AREA: 950 SQ M
IMAGE: DENNIS GILBERT

The architects have successfully integrated new staff rooms in an elegantly proportioned but uncompromisingly modern three-level building between Grade I and Grade II listed Brighton College buildings. The somewhat enclosed external spaces have been opened up by deftly repositioning an archway entrance and using the site's changes in level to form a very popular outdoor performance space. The connection between new and old is made with delicate strip of glazing. There is a commendable 'rightness' about the building in its setting.

Skidelsky Building
Eastern Road, Brighton, East Sussex

KIRKLAND FRASER MOOR

CLIENT: BRIGHTON COLLEGE
STRUCTURAL ENGINEER: DAVID DEXTER & ASSOCIATES
SERVICES ENGINEER: ATELIER 10
CONTRACTOR: BUXTON BUILDING CONTRACTORS
CONTRACT VALUE: CONFIDENTIAL
DATE OF COMPLETION: OCTOBER 2010
GROSS INTERNAL AREA: 1,025 SQ M
IMAGE: KILLIAN O'SULLIVAN

As the first of nine new buildings in the same architects' masterplan for Brighton College Independent School, the Skidelsky building provides new classrooms, a laboratory and common rooms. The client wanted an economic, almost industrial feel, to the new Lower School building to act as a decanter to allow other parts of the masterplan to be developed. It is made from almost black, in reference to the local flint and is naturally ventilated through large Douglas Fir hinged panelling which characterise the façade.

Toot Rise
Toot Rock, Pett Level, East Sussex

NICK EVANS ARCHITECTS

CLIENT: NICK EVANS
STRUCTURAL ENGINEER: PRICE AND MYERS
CONTRACTOR: ASHLEY DEVELOPMENTS
CONTRACT VALUE: CONFIDENTIAL
DATE OF COMPLETION: JANUARY 2012
GROSS INTERNAL AREA: 208 SQ M
IMAGE: SIR PAUL SMITH

This simple modern house has sea or rural views through 360 degrees. A high proportion of the walls and roof is glazed in order to maximise the view and producing fascinating shadow-play throughout the house. In turn the house is highly insulated and, wherever possible, sustainable resources and renewable energy systems have been incorporated. The house was designed to comprise small components, which were easy to manoeuvre for the small local builder, working in close collaboration with the architect/owner.

Watts Gallery
Down Lane, Compton, Guildford, Surrey

ZMMA

CLIENT: THE WATTS GALLERY
STRUCTURAL ENGINEER: ADRIAN COX ASSOCIATES
SERVICES ENGINEER: HARLEY HADDOW
CONTRACTOR: BLENHEIM HOUSE CONTRACTS
CONTRACT VALUE: £4.5 MILLION
DATE OF COMPLETION: JUNE 2011
GROSS INTERNAL AREA: 1,208 SQ M
IMAGE: DAVID GRANDORGE
WINNER OF RIBA REGIONAL CONSERVATION AWARD

The site is significant to English Heritage (who rate it Grade II*) because, unusually, it is a purpose-built gallery for the collection of a single artist; still more so because GF Watts commissioned the building in 1904 shortly before his own death to house his own works. The original buildings were of mass concrete and brick walls with roughcast render externally and lime render inside. The new architects made clear distinctions between preserving the best of the existing fabric and making major interventions; so no fakery, no pastiche.

Bermondsey Island
Abbey Street, Bermondsey, London SE1

URBAN SALON

CLIENT: IGLOO REGENERATION
STRUCTURAL ENGINEER: HEYNE TILLETT STEEL
SERVICES ENGINEER: BSEC
CONTRACTOR: ALLENBUILD SOUTH EAST
CONTRACT VALUE: CONFIDENTIAL
DATE OF COMPLETION: NOVEMBER 2011
GROSS INTERNAL AREA: 1,217 SQ M
IMAGE: GARETH GARDNER

This is a modest development providing affordable rented flats and a commercial unit on a small island site. The architects have chosen to reflect the differing urban natures, on either sides of the site. The busy road side elevations are clad in a precise, dark, hard Tilebrick, punctuated by dark framed windows. The quieter sides splay out in a series of white rendered walls, with white framed patio doors, behind the vertical struts of balconies, which form a sort of yashmak for privacy and shading.

Bow Riverside
London. E3

ADAMS & SUTHERLAND

CLIENT: BRITISH WATERWAYS
STRUCTURAL ENGINEER: HALCROW GROUP
CONTRACTOR: MAY GURNEY
CONTRACT VALUE: £2.4 MILLION
DATE OF COMPLETION: AUGUST 2011
GROSS INTERNAL AREA: 2,177 SQ M
IMAGE: LONDON CYCLING CAMPAIGN

The new footbridge and suspended walkway running beneath the bridge together provide a route for pedestrians and cyclists, allowing them to connect safely across this busy East End neighbourhood. The zig-zagging form allows the necessary height for river traffic to pass under the bridge. The simple steel structure is clad in an undulating series of vertical timbers that provide a secure barrier, but also blur the distinction between towpath and bridge to create a new place that intimately engages with its riverside setting.

BSkyB Sky Studios
Harlequin Avenue, Isleworth TW8

ARUP ASSOCIATES

CLIENT: BRITISH SKY BROADCASTING/STANHOPE
STRUCTURAL ENGINEER: ARUP
SERVICES ENGINEER: ARUP
CONTRACTOR: LEND LEASE
CONTRACT VALUE: CONFIDENTIAL
DATE OF COMPLETION: JUNE 2011
GROSS INTERNAL AREA: 21,442 SQ M
IMAGE: CHRISTIAN RICHTERS
WINNER OF RIBA LONDON SUSTAINABILITY AWARD

The building is organised horizontally to reflect the three key functions: 'make' – the studios on the lower levels; 'shape' – production and editing on the middle floors and 'share' – the transmission platforms on the top floor. The façades feature the natural ventilation chimneys, whereby the studios benefit from a natural ventilation system which is driven by waste heat from the studio lights. The result is a Factory for Television that sets the international benchmark for sustainability in high energy-use buildings and satisfies the client's carbon reduction commitments.

Canada Water Library
Surrey Quays Road, London SE16

CZWG

CLIENT: LONDON BOROUGH OF SOUTHWARK
STRUCTURAL ENGINEER: AKT II
SERVICES ENGINEER: HOARE LEA CONSULTING ENGINEERS
CONTRACTOR: ISG JACKSON
CONTRACT VALUE: £14.1 MILLION
DATE OF COMPLETION: NOVEMBER 2011
GROSS INTERNAL AREA: 2,900 SQ M
IMAGE: TIM CROCKER

The library was built as the civic centerpiece for the regeneration of the area around Canada Water and as a focus for the community. Southwark Council, who are building libraries while other boroughs are closing theirs, saw that by adding a performance space, education and meeting rooms and a café to the Library, they were better serving the needs and aspirations of their residents. And it seems to be working. The perforated anodized aluminium cladding shimmers in the sunlight and mimics the ripples of the water it sits beside.

Crown Woods College
Bexley Road Eltham, London SE9

NICHOLAS HARE ARCHITECTS
CLIENT: GREENWICH COUNTY COUNCIL
STRUCTURAL ENGINEER: BDP
SERVICES ENGINEER: BDP
CONTRACTOR: BALFOUR BEATTY
CONTRACT VALUE: £41 MILLION
DATE OF COMPLETION: MAY 2011
GROSS INTERNAL AREA: 16,447 SQ M
IMAGE: PETER DURANT

This schools project breaks down the size of an enormous and struggling comprehensive school. It is arranged into three separate schools of about 450 pupils and a Sixth Form college, who share the resources of a central administration, Arts, Music and Sports Centres. There is also a separate Special Needs section whose design has a calming influence on behaviour. The construction – brickwork and pre-cast concrete walkway covers, with simple, elegant glazed infill panels – is hard-wearing and the elevations are pleasingly consistent, but also suitably varied.

Four Seasons Hotel Spa
Hamilton Place, Park Lane, London W1

ERIC PARRY ARCHITECTS
CLIENT: CONFIDENTIAL
STRUCTURAL ENGINEER: ADAMS KARA TAYLOR
SERVICES ENGINEER: INDUSTRIAL DESIGN ASSOCIATES
CONTRACTOR: BECK INTERIORS
CONTRACT VALUE: CONFIDENTIAL
DATE OF COMPLETION: MARCH 2011
GROSS INTERNAL AREA: 1,800 SQ M
IMAGE: EDMUND SUMNER

The architects have added a two-storey roof-top extension which has architecturally completed what had previously appeared as an unfinished building. The concept of the extension as a 'hat' – the lower storey set back under an overhanging brim, the upper volume a shallow vaulted roof – satisfies a number of criteria which are particular to both the existing building and its location. The leading edge of the brim, echoing the form of the building below, has a dark soffit, its gloss finish reflecting street level activity.

Mint Hotel Tower of London
Pepys Street, London EC3

BENNETTS ASSOCIATES

CLIENT: MINT HOTEL
STRUCTURAL ENGINEER: BURO HAPPOLD
SERVICES ENGINEER: AECOM
INTERIOR DESIGN: WOODS BAGOT
CONTRACTOR: LAING O'ROURKE
CONTRACT VALUE: £72 MILLION
DATE OF COMPLETION: JANUARY 2010
GROSS INTERNAL AREA: 28,000 SQ M
IMAGE: EDMUND SUMNER

This 583 bed hotel occupies a tight urban site and reinstates the ancient street pattern of its part of the City. A two-storey colonnade forms a covered arrival and drop-off area that allows visitors to see directly into the central court of the building; the seven-storey stone-clad hotel block is arranged around this courtyard. Perched above this block is the zinc-clad 'sky lounge'. The hotel's carefully considered approach to sustainability achieves a 40% improvement on the usual standards for hotels.

National Maritime Museum
Sammy Ofer Wing
Romney Road, Greenwich, London SE10

PURCELL MILLER TRITTON

CLIENT: NATIONAL MARITIME MUSEUM
STRUCTURAL ENGINEER: ADAMS KARA TAYLOR
SERVICES ENGINEER: MOTT MACDONALD FULCRUM
CONTRACTOR: LEND LEASE
CONTRACT VALUE: CONFIDENTIAL — (£36.5 MILLION)
DATE OF COMPLETION: JULY 2011
GROSS INTERNAL AREA: 3,345 SQ M
IMAGE: NATIONAL MARITIME MUSEUM

When appointed five years ago the new Director realised the enormous potential for the Museum to attract more visitors by opening up the side of the Museum facing the park. Visitors are now led down a series of ramped gardens to the strong, identifiable entrance. There is a generous foyer area with the café, shop, introductory exhibition and the usual information areas. Stairs, within the lofty atrium, lead down to an enormous special Exhibition Gallery below. The entrance is lit by elaborate roof lanterns, which heighten the experience.

Painted House
London NW11

JONATHAN WOOLF ARCHITECTS

CLIENT: PRIVATE
STRUCTURAL ENGINEER: BUILT ENGINEERS
SERVICES ENGINEER: SVM CONSULTING ENGINEERS
CONTRACTOR: HEIGHTS (UK) INVESTMENTS
CONTRACT VALUE: CONFIDENTIAL
DATE OF COMPLETION: OCTOBER 2010
GROSS INTERNAL AREA: 770 SQ M
IMAGE: HELENE BINET

The Painted House is a model house: aesthetically, environmentally and sociologically. This pair of 'semis' is now home to the client and three generations of his extended family of eleven. The two houses have largely been rebuilt but certain elevations have been retained. Inside plastered surfaces are bright, downstairs the floors are screed, upstairs ply, and throughout the painted joinery is warm grey. It is this homogenization that successfully draws one's attention to the particular size and shape of each space.

South Norwood Hill Children's Centre
Cypress Road, South Norwood, London SE25

ERECT ARCHITECTURE

CLIENT: THE CYPRESS SCHOOLS
STRUCTURAL ENGINEER: BUILT ENGINEERS
SERVICES ENGINEER: AUSTEN ASSOCIATES
CONTRACTOR: HILIFE CONSTRUCTION CO
CONTRACT VALUE: £715,000
DATE OF COMPLETION: APRIL 2011
GROSS INTERNAL AREA: 276 SQ M
IMAGE: ERECT ARCHITECTURE

The old school was dark and unloved but it has been retained and transformed, its size doubled by wrapping new accommodation and terraces around it, re-orientating it and linking it to its wooded site. The limited range of materials, timber and brick, used in a very coherent, yet flexible way informs the building's charming character. Inside a succession of pitched roofs, with the timber trusses exposed, scale and zone the nursery school and the multipurpose room. New roof lights let daylight into the deep plan.

St Christopher's the Hall School, Reception Block
Bromley

RALA

CLIENT: CONFIDENTIAL
STRUCTURAL ENGINEER: OCSC
SERVICES ENGINEER: J.M. NASH
CONTRACTOR: 8BUILD
CONTRACT VALUE: CONFIDENTIAL
DATE OF COMPLETION: JUNE 2011
GROSS INTERNAL AREA: 495 SQ M
IMAGE: ROSS LAMBIE

The Reception Block takes the form of a little Corbusian pavilion. It achieves two storeys, within the planning height constraints, by cleverly setting back the raised middle of the first floor hall with clerestorey windows. This enabled the school to build a second hall above, for general use. There are lots of child-friendly and enticing details, like the library-cum-book snug that cantilevers into the double-height group space, and the windows at different heights for everyone.

St Paul's Cathedral
St Paul's Churchyard London EC4

MARTIN STANCLIFFE ARCHITECTS / PURCELL

CLIENT: THE DEAN & CHAPTER OF ST PAUL'S CATHEDRAL
STRUCTURAL ENGINEER: ALAN BAXTER ASSOCIATES
SERVICES ENGINEER: ENG DESIGN
ARCHAEOLOGICAL: JOHN SCHOFIELD
CONTRACTOR: ST PAUL'S CATHEDRAL WORKS DEPARTMENT
CONTRACT VALUE: £32 MILLION
DATE OF COMPLETION: FEBRUARY 2012
IMAGE: RICS
WINNER OF ENGLISH HERITAGE AWARD FOR SUSTAINING THE HISTORIC ENVIRONMENT

For most historic buildings, the continuing maintenance and repair of their fabric is an ongoing requirement so the opportunity to address these issues in a cohesive manner seldom arises. Here the approach is based on painstaking research and covers the cleaning and restoration of the interior and exterior, the removal of many twentieth-century accretions, the opening up of the crypt and the subtle integration of accessibility requirements. This holistic and thoughtful approach to the care of an important building sets new benchmarks in the conservation of our historic fabric.

Tea Building
Shoreditch High Street, London E1

ALLFORD HALL MONAGHAN MORRIS

CLIENT: DERWENT LONDON
STRUCTURAL ENGINEER: AKERA ENGINEERING
SERVICES ENGINEER: PETER DEER AND ASSOCIATES;
CUNDALL JOHNSTON & PARTNERS
GRAPHIC DESIGN: STUDIO MYERSCOUGH
CONTRACTOR: THORNTON PARTNERSHIP
CONTRACT VALUE: CONFIDENTIAL
DATE OF COMPLETION: JANUARY 2012
GROSS INTERNAL AREA: 26,000 SQ M
IMAGE: ROB PARISH

The block consists of a number of different late Victorian buildings. A programme of low-cost fabric and servicing upgrades has gradually been implemented over ten years. New architectural interventions appropriate to the user – cafes, offices, galleries, clubs and hotel – include a shipping container used as a reception and a corten extension rising out of the top of a Victorian pub. The result is a quirky alternative to the traditional work environment, further developed by the fit-outs carried out by the various architects working within the stewardship of AHMM.

THE ROYAL GOLD MEDAL

Elizabeth Walder
MA FRSA

The Royal Gold Medal was established by the RIBA in 1848, and is still awarded and celebrated today. It was conceived as a result of a conversation between the then President of the RIBA, Earl de Grey, and Prince Albert.

The idea for a Gold Medal had come about in 1846, twelve years after the foundation of the RIBA. Originally, it was to be awarded to the winner of a competition to encourage young architects to design 'a building suitable and practical to house the Institute and its daily operations' – an idea that received royal approval from Buckingham Palace. Eleven designs were submitted, but – according to the RIBA's centenary history – 'they missed the mark so entirely: they were, most of them, so grandiose and expensive – in short, they so widely disregarded the conditions imposed, that the medal was not awarded. This fiasco sealed the fate of the junior members of the profession in regard to the medal and it was decided to award it in future not to the immature work of the young but in recognition of the actual achievements of the older men [sic].' (In fact, to date, shockingly, no woman has won the medal in her own right.)

Earl de Grey's fresh approach was communicated to Queen Victoria via Prince Albert. It was agreed that the medal should be 'conferred on some distinguished architect for work of high merit, or on some distinguished person whose work has promoted either directly or indirectly the advancement of architecture'. This has remained the basis of the criteria to this day.

The RIBA commissioned William Wyon, Chief Engraver of the Royal Mint, to execute the medal. The Vice-President of the RIBA, Ambrose Poynter, designed the reverse, showing a laurel wreath encircling text and the RIBA's coat of arms. The name of the winner is inscribed around the edge of the medal. Today the Royal Gold Medal is still made by the Royal Mint. As the gift of the monarch, it shares a coveted status with twenty-four other Royal Prize Medals awarded annually by Her Majesty The Queen. As originally conceived, previous winners include architects, engineers, historians, writers and theorists (see pages 217–219).

Nominations for Royal Gold Medallists are made by members of the RIBA in the third quarter of the year prior to the year of the award. Names are considered by a distinguished panel chaired by the President of the RIBA and including architects and non-architects from the United Kingdom and overseas. One name is presented to Her Majesty for approval, and the winner is announced in October. The formal presentation is held the following February.

This year's Honours Committee, which chooses the Medallist and the International and Honorary Fellows (see pages 190 and 198), comprised the following:

ANGELA BRADY
RIBA President

NIALL MCLAUGHLIN

PETER CLEGG

SARAH WIGGLESWORTH

YVONNE FARRELL

PROFESSOR ADRIAN FORTY

Herman Hertzberger
The Royal Gold Medal Citation

Niall McLaughlin

For the Dutch architect Herman Hertzberger the structure of a building is not an end in itself, it is literally the framework for the life that goes on inside it, a life that is determined by its users. This goes for a school, a home or an office – all building-types he has transformed in a fifty year career in architecture.

Herman Hertzberger was one of the leaders in the movement away from functionalism in the mid-twentieth century. Influenced by semiotics, linguistics and structural rationalism he sought to identify an underlying order in a building's construction that is not related purely to its function. He saw this as analogous to the deep grammatical structures in language explored by Claude Lévi-Strauss; just as grammar is brought to life in speech, so the fundamental tectonic order in buildings is given social meaning by the way in which they are inhabited. Because for Hertzberger inhabitation is all.

Structurally Hertzberger's buildings are characterised by a clear articulation of the supporting lattice. This creates a series of cellular zones within which minor elements like sills, benches and thresholds are used to prompt human occupation. His debt to anthropology is manifested in his particular concern for these defined territories which are both joined and separated by liminal or threshold elements. These 'in-between' pieces set up a dialogue between adjacent spatial orders as well as encourage social interaction.

As a discipline architecture is a continuous unfolding dialogue between tectonic organisation and social meaning. The user of a building is encouraged to change its underlying organisation by occupying it creatively. So although the construction does not in itself have meaning, it creates a space where meaning can be defined.

Hertzberger took his spiritual leadership from the work of Aldo van Eyck, one of the team X (along with Jaap Bakema, Giancarlo De Carlo, and Alison and Peter Smithson) – the movement which led to both structuralism and the new brutalism. Between 1959 and 1963, with Bakema and Van Eyck, he edited the journal Forum, which became the mouth-piece for structuralism in architecture. In his books, based in part on his lectures at Delft University of Technology, Lessons for Students in Architecture (1991), Space and the Architect: Lessons in Architecture 2 (1999) and Space and Learning (2008) he not only outlined his ideas and principles, he also discussed his sources of inspiration such as the Egyptian pyramids, the ancient Greek theatre at Epidaurus, the benches in the Parc Güell of Antoni Gaudi, the Pueblos in Arizona, the Piazza Anfiteatro in Lucca, Diocletian's Palace in Split, as well as Le Corbusier's early work. In one of his earliest buildings the Student Housing in Amsterdam (1959-66), designed while he was still a student himself at the Polytechnic of Delft, his admiration for the roof zone of the Unité d'Habitation in Marseille is clear. Meanwhile his pre-

occupation with the city as the highest manifestation of the socialisation of mankind is evidenced by his co-founding and acting as the first Dean of the Berlage Institute in Amsterdam, an architecture school set up as a laboratory for urbanism and the built environment.

His first completed building, however, was an industrial laundry in Amsterdam. This he perched on top of an early twentieth-century building, marking the start of a lifelong concern with extending the life of buildings, by others and his own, for example the Vredenburg Music Centre in Utrecht (1973-78) which is currently being rebuilt from the outside-in. That said, his primary concern is not for a building's form but its structure and its inner world and workings. Every Hertzberger project contains a strong idea, and his principles are best illustrated by the many schools that he and his studio have built in the last fifty years. The stairs and corridors are not isolated elements but are essential to the life that fills the building; to see and being seen are the first steps towards a more satisfactory and fulfilling existence. His celebrated Montessori School in Delft (1960-66), an ever ongoing work in progress, rethought the way classrooms are laid out – L-shaped rooms creating different zones, all linked by wide, zig-zagging corridors. The images of children sitting, conversing and playing on broad wooden steps in the Apollo Schools in Amsterdam and in the conversation pit in the Delft school have inspired many architects of schools across northern Europe and across the decades.

Centraal Beheer Apeldoorn (1968–72)

His early masterpiece is an exemplary workplace known as Centraal Beheer (1968-72), offices for an insurance company in Apeldoorn, a workers' village based on a three-dimensional grid, put together and inhabited with bee-like assiduousness. The larger structural matrix is interwoven with smaller strands inviting occupation; workers have even been invited by the firm to introduce their own pieces of furniture. Centraal Beheer is most notable for its success in empowering the individual, even if it is sometimes at the expense of economy.

The textile character of Hertzberger's early buildings is strongly reminiscent of Frank Lloyd Wright's Larkin

Administration Building, which itself leads us back to Le Duc and Semper. In that sense, Hertzberger's ideas, interpreted from innovative 20th century disciplines, are embedded in an older architectural order. In Utrecht and Apeldoorn and in the Ministry of Social Affairs and Employment in The Hague (1979-90) the use of standardised elements is clear both in plan and in elevation. His social welfare building was one of the first to develop the idea of the internal street, or elongated atrium, to encourage social interaction in the workplace and to get light into all the rooms. Another trope of late-modernism, the over-sailing all-embracing roof, was developed for the Chassé Theatre, Breda (1992-95) whose fly towers, auditoria and foyers are all tucked under a split undulating roof-form.

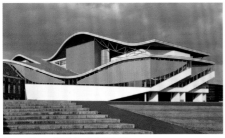

Chasse Concert Hall, Breda (1992–95)

Throughout his architecture Hertzberger employs a grammar of elements that enables people to define their own habitat within the structure. For him all buildings should adapt themselves to different needs. This is best expressed in his housing work, as is his humanity as an architect. In the early experimental skeleton houses Diagoon, Delft (1969-70) the indefinite plan allows the purpose of each space to be designated by the occupants, while the section allows for diagonal views. The LiMa residential building in Berlin (1982-86) extends the principle of flexibility to mass housing, with the buildings arranged around a sun-filled courtyard and communal staircases forming vertical streets. And in Middelburg in 2004, he turned his attention to the very Dutch issue of living with water and designed an experimental floating house, which, in theory at least, can be re-orientated to catch the sun.

Floating Villa, Middelburg (2002–04)

In his later work he constantly re-visits the themes addressed in his earlier writings: Coda Shelter for Culture in Apeldoorn (2000-04), with its courtyard, its inviting glazing

Faculty of Science, University of Utrecht (2006–11)

to the street and its undulating interior landscape; Waternet Head Office in Amsterdam (2000–05), two towers with their tapering ribbons of glazing, which re-rehearse the ideas of the open workplace, the central social space, and a building's capacity to accept change; while in the Faculty of Science at the University of Utrecht (2006-2011) he translates the cuboid circulation and break-out platforms separated by light wells of Centraal Beheer, into the more fluid architectural language of the early twenty-first century.

What Hertzberger wants is an architecture that can be interpreted and used by the inhabitants in many ways. He is an advocate of the open society in which encounters are not planned but occur in a spontaneous, natural manner. His architecture facilitates such a use and stresses more the sight- and contact-lines than the representational character of the facades. For him architecture is not only a social activity but should also stimulate the user into finding his or her place in society. It has to give meaning and it has to be able to receive meaning. Hertzberger's architecture always has a strong didactic component. This can also be said for his writings. His architecture contain lessons that have nothing to do with representation or image-making but that have much to do with the manner he perceives the way people live together. His architecture permits a flexible use and can always accommodate the unexpected.

Hertzberger borrows the word 'polyvalent' from chemistry to propose that buildings are open to multiple modes of inhabitation over time. In doing this he admits our changing needs, but insists on the continuity of deeper patterns of dwelling. This was a powerful challenge to modernism's linking of form to use. Although he never accepted that flexibility was intrinsic to functionalism, he did resist the idea that building form is in itself significant. In so doing he set architects the challenge of finding constructional rhythms to frame the fundamental patterns of human inhabitation. This was not only a powerful criticism of early modernist assumptions, but it also set contemporary architecture a stern challenge.

Medallist Peter Cook wrote in 1967: 'Architecture is a social art, the value of a building must lie chiefly in its ability to create environment out of human situations. The architect can set himself the limit of the existing pattern, but most good architects would not be content with this.' Hertzberger has never been content with conventional thinking; despite the continuity of his architecture he is constantly re-inventing his own solutions.

Herman Hertzberger
in conversation with Tony Chapman

TC I'm going to start off by talking to you about why you have only once built outside Europe – the dormitory in Japan – why is that? You are an international architect of international repute, why aren't you building all over the world?

HH Well, people from Japan came to me because they had a factory in Holland and they thought that in Holland they make things small and they didn't want to spend much money so they thought they should have the architect who makes small things. That was the very simple, practical reason. And then I got to know these people, the YKK Firm, all the trousers all over the world have YKK zippers but they also make all sorts of building materials. And so they asked me to make a dormitory in Japan. Fantastic job!

TC And you've never worked in Britain and yet it's so close geographically and spiritually to the Netherlands, why is that?

HH No. I should ask you that. I don't know about the situation now but maybe they might not be interested in my type of work which is actually different from the work of most of my colleagues. Look now through the windows over there is Ben van Berkel's UN Studio – so they may go one door further.

TC Skip a generation.

HH Yes. I worked a lot in Germany and Italy so with Japan that's the three countries that formed the Axis Powers. Anyway they ask me to build, so I do.

TC You are known across the whole world not only for your architecture but for your books and your teaching. Your writing is rather like your buildings, isn't it? – you keep re-visiting them, you will do version of a book and then come back to it.

HH Actually I am a sort of teacher and I'm always inclined to find out things for myself, but I use others to find it out things for me too. When I was professor at Delft we gave talks every fortnight. When I say we, it was also Aldo van Eyck and others. It was a major series of talks, always with a full house. I had the idea not to just show my own work – it's a funny thing that architects are always giving talks on their own work, and they say 'this is this and that is that…' and for the students that doesn't work. So what you may say we invented was the idea not to make a course in architecture history but a sort of history of modernity. So 50% of the work in my own first book, which was the result of all these talks, is not my own work. I use my own work just to illustrate the book but most of the illustrations are other architects'. And also 50% of the illustrations are modern and 50% historical.

TC But of course it's important to your own work as well, because you were drawing on those examples.

HH Of course, of course. Exactly what you say. For me I was my best student I think. I worked very hard to prepare these talks and I learnt a lot by just asking myself, why am I doing this and is there a better example to explain what I wanted to say? So that was my first book, Lessons for Students in Architecture. And then after that I wrote a second book to pinpoint some things a little further and to outline the things that I learnt since the first book. And then came a third book on schools, because I designed so many schools – I think we designed something like 50 or 60 schools, of which 30 were actually built.

TC I want to come on to discussing particular building types later but I just want to pursue this idea of history – obviously continuity with the past is very important to you but the danger is that of course you slide into historicism, you're making historical references.

HH No this danger doesn't exist. This is the danger of historians. They imply that history was better than modernity, I never did. For me modernity was number one and I only pointed out that certain principles of modernity are not completely modern, they have been used before, although in a slightly different way, maybe in a very different way. And actually this is also the idea of structuralism, that when it comes to new styles it is only superficially new, or let's say, it's only new in the sense that the emphasis is different. But the fact is they are mainly the same.

TC Because every architect has a context and that is partly geography and it's partly history but it's about place and it's about the past – but you mustn't be the slave of that context?

HH But modern architects, modern schools of architecture, they don't know what history is.

TC Is that the fault of the architectural education system?

HH Yes it's the architectural education system but it's also our society which is only interested in the use of the new and they forget that the idea of new doesn't exist. It's just a new shoot of the same thing. The fact is that architects are often missing the point, there is, in my opinion, no deep thinking behind their work. So I'm not saying that architects are wrong, the only thing I want to say is that I think a little bit differently. And there are not many architects, if you were to ask me which architects are in my family of thinking, I would be in difficulty because actually I don't know. Architects are very outwardly directed and they make beautiful things for the sake of beauty and there's nothing wrong with that but it's not my cup of tea.

TC You say that you don't feel other architects agree with you and yet you have had an enormous influence on other architects.

HH Isn't that fantastic? It means that you're doing something right. Did I say I disagree with these architects? I said they are doing something else. They make beautiful buildings and sometimes I look in these magazines and I say 'My God how can you make such a beautiful thing!' But it's a different profession.

TC Perhaps I can just draw your attention to your predecessor as Royal Gold Medallist David Chipperfield. He has made a beautiful television studio in Glasgow that uses your principles of stepped communal spaces – it's almost entirely communal except when you have to go into a studio, but it's a stepped building, you climb up through it, there's a progression through it, a promenade architecturale if you like.

HH So it works. That's fantastic. I mean this is how culture works. I learnt the basis of what I think from Aldo van Eyck, from Rietfeld and in the first place from Le Corbusier and they put the seeds in the soil and I'm trying to continue this. But it's really the best news you can bring me when you say that this goes on, that it works. And I must say, I see more and more inner spaces that are treated like streets and like places and the idea that making something communal is somehow frightening – this idea of 'where is my territory? I want my door to close', you know, all that is going to fade away. By the way I am not the first one to make a big office landscape – although I always say that Centraal Beheer is not really an office landscape anyway, I always added the word articulated to it, an articulated landscape. But there were already before some landscapes, some places, where people sat in large spaces and I found out that they still work too. Foster was doing that at exactly the time that I was doing Centraal Beheer here, with his famous building Willis Faber in Ipswich.

TC With your theatres the foyer is an extension of the street: bringing the city into the theatre and the theatre onto the street.

HH Exactly. I try to make the foyers as streets. I try to make as many conditions or situations where it's possible for people to look at each other, to see hmm what's that new look, or – oh, she is with someone else – that is part of the function of the theatre. Of course, the main function is the play but it's also seeing the state of affairs. In that sense we sometimes call it the living room of the city. In cities too there are places that you can call the living room, where things happen.

TC There is nothing more theatrical than a school, they are the most theatrical of buildings. I want to go back to talk about the Apollo schools in Amsterdam because they use the idea of the amphitheatre.

HH That started it for me. I found out there that this makes the whole school into one family.

TC And then there's the question of the individual and the community.

HH Absolutely, they are the two poles of the way I work. They are also the two poles of language and speech. The use of language is individual, people can use the language in their own way and yet the phenomenon is that you still understand what the other is saying even though he maybe uses syntax in a different way, it's still understandable. So we all use this communal language in our own way, and that's the basis of my work.

TC We haven't really talked about what structuralism is, what it means to you.

HH To explain structuralism would need an hour but if we compare it with chess playing you could say that there are rules and there is what you do with the rules. So all chess players, from small boys to crack players, have the same rules and they play with the same rules but some do more

Music Palace Vrendenberg, Utrecht (1973–78)

with them, some do very personal things and others are just following the rules. The idea of structuralism is derived from language theory: the idea that we all use the same language which is the rules of the game but we all use these rules in a different way. So could we maybe use this idea in architecture by starting from a common thing and leave room for people to interpret that in their own way? So what I am trying to do is make what you call structure – which is not the same thing as making a span that is also structure – but structure is keeping things together, that's the idea of structure, to keep things together. That's the idea of language as well so you can call it structure. Could we make buildings that have a structure, that leave a part that is sort of open or vulnerable to everything, which is a sort of competence, which then we could leave to people to fill in, to perform in their own way? So you can call structure also the framework. But not just in the construction sense.

TC I know you once remarked on the fact that Berlioz always refused to learn to play the piano because he was afraid of endlessly repeating chord sequences in his compositions because they come so naturally on the piano. Is that what you think about computers: that the results are too predictable?

HH That's another thing. The story about Berlioz playing the piano and the hands going into chords, it's like pitfalls, you fall into the same chord. I play the piano myself and so I know how it is – and the more handy you are, and I'm not very handy just handy enough – the easier you make these chords, the more you are repeating what you have already found. So I'm not complaining about the computer but it does choose your way of working. It's all about the person who is sitting in front of the computer, it's not that thing, that machine that does the harm, it's the persons that are working with it who do the harm, although mostly they are very good. But the working method changes because they offer me in one minute 50 possibilities. It works in a different way with drawings but the result could be the same I think.

Actually there is this famous story of Michelangelo and he was cutting a piece of stone and a beautiful woman comes out of the stone. And then this passer-by asks him, how did you know there was this beautiful woman in that stone? So with cutting you must really know what you are cutting. Le Corbusier calls it the patient search – you keep trying and you say this is not what I want – because beforehand you have an idea of a certain quality, so more or less you know what you are looking for but not exactly.

TC What does winning prizes like the Royal Gold Medal mean to you?

HH Getting this prize means much for me. I try just to keep normal but it's for me a small miracle that my not really sexy architecture is recognised, that the idea of, you may call it, social architecture is recognised. It gives me hope. There is a very funny discussion on one of these social network sites where people talk with each other: they like something or they don't like it. Some say they dislike the idea that I get this prize, they say, 'Wow, this is absolutely nonsense, this man is not like Herzog and de Meuron and Mies van der Rohe'. And other people who like it say, 'Yes, but he at least is a

Centraal Beheer, Apeldoorn (1968–72)

NHL University, Leeuwarden (2004–10)

social architect and we might need that in architecture'. So recognition of the point I try to push forward is a fantastic thing. In that sense it changes my life, but it does not change my life in the sense that I feel like another person now.

TC And I think those who are sceptical should go to one of your Montessori schools. I have been to three of them and to see that calm and yet energy in the same space, at the same time – that is a remarkable thing.

HH Yes but the discussion is then, is that part of architecture or not?

TC Of course it is.

HH Because for most people architecture is considered to be something else, something connected to beauty, connected to order, that sort of thing. For me I'm quite at home in architectural history, I know my Palladio and Alberti and Brunelleschi and Bernini and I learn from all those people. But I think in our time we must add something else. These people made spaces where people could come together and have a feeling of belonging: that is the big thing that all these classical architects, in my opinion, did. And this is something which is not lost in our time, but it's understated.

TC You're approaching 80 and you told me how you had restructured the practice and yet you are probably busier than ever – so will you ever retire from architecture do you think?

HH There is a famous book which is discussed everywhere at this moment in Holland. It's written by a brain specialist and it says something like, 'I am my brain'. It's very materialistic because it denies free will. But I don't know, it really is a question of how long your brain will help you to think. I'm dependent, completely dependent, on how long that machine will still run. But if I could make my own decision, I would never stop working.

De Eilanden School, Amsterdam

Coda Shelter for Culture, Apeldoorn (2004–11)

Montessori School, Delft (1960–66)

Ministry of Social Affairs and Employment, The Hague

Presikhaven School, Arnhem

Faculty of Science University of Utrecht (2006-11)

Apolloscholen, Amsterdam (1980–83)

THE RIBA
INTERNATIONAL
FELLOWSHIPS

Throughout its history, the RIBA has honoured men and women who have made a major contribution to the world of design and, in particular, architecture. Any architect outside the United Kingdom who is not a UK citizen, has a demonstrable interest in the objectives of the RIBA, and exhibits distinction and breadth of contribution to architecture may be elected an International Fellow of the RIBA. The lifetime honour, conferred annually, allows recipients to use the initials Int FRIBA after their name. Prior to 2006, such people were elected Honorary Fellows; in 2006, with the creation of the new honour, all architect Honorary Fellows, including non-UK surviving Royal Gold Medallists, were made RIBA International Fellows.

Of the seven architects made International Fellows in 2012, two work in partnership. They come from four different countries, and their work not only represents the spirit of their countries, but transcends it to become truly international in its reference and influence.

This year's RIBA International Fellows were chosen by the Honours Committee, which also selects the Royal Gold Medallist and the RIBA Honorary Fellows (see pages 182–189 and 198–205).

For the list of committee members, see page 182.

Atelier Bow-Wow: Momoyo Kaijima and Yoshiharu Tsukamoto

Japan

Atelier Bow-Wow's work in Tokyo defines new urban and architectural typologies, shunning any particular style and instead developing a kind of accidental urban vernacular. Atelier Bow-Wow was founded in 1992, its name referring to a pack of dogs running, barking, sniffing around their city in search of ever-new encounters and adventures.

Momoyo Kaijima and Yoshiharu Tsukamoto have been described as urban detectives, scouring the urban fabric, seeking out examples of buildings that occupy spaces left when the economic tide goes out. The result of their research is a kind of architectural sampling: the buildings they make can serve many different functions, such as sewage disposal and sports hall.

The results of their investigation, which began in 1991 and identified 70 examples of 'da-me' or 'no good' architecture, were published in 2001 in Made in Tokyo. This can be read as a guidebook to the ordinary, everyday architecture of the post-bubble city, but it also has a wider resonance by suggesting ways in which we can begin to deal with our shrinking cities.

Their 1999 Mini House was built on land set aside for the new Kan-8 Loop Road, which cut across the grid and created many left over spaces. They theoretically populated these with examples of 'pet architecture': small ad hoc, customisable buildings. This strategy resulted in built projects such as Gae House (2001), and their house and studio (2005), with its permeable interiors and mingling of public and private spaces.

Momoyo Kaijima graduated in 1991 from the Japan Women's University, after which she obtained her master's degree at the Tokyo Institute of Technology. Yoshiharu Tsukamoto obtained his PhD in 1994 from the Tokyo Institute of Technology, after studying in France at the Paris- Belleville School of Architecture. Both are currently professors and at the top of their game as architects.

IMAGES: ATELIER BOW-WOW

Mado Building

Carlos Ferrater
Spain

Carlos Ferrater's practice, the Office of Architecture in Barcelona, is a partnership between experience and youth. Set up in 2006 and led by the renowned, innovative Catalan architect Carlos Ferrater, it aimed to bring in the youthful ideas of Xavier Martí, Lucía Ferrater, Borja Ferrater and Núria Ayala. The practice is not only concerned with construction projects – its work is complemented and enriched by teaching and academic research.

Carlos Ferrater was born in Barcelona in 1944, has a doctorate in architecture and teaches at the Polytechnic University of Catalonia. His portfolio begins in 1971 with Instant City, his intricately interlinked inflatable tented structures in Ibiza.

He designed three city blocks in the Olympic Village of Barcelona at Parc de Mar, and the Olympic Village on the edge of the city at Vall d'Hebron. These not only regenerated two post-industrial areas of the city but are among the best examples of post-Olympic legacy anywhere in the world.

Carlos Ferrater's Botanical Garden in Barcelona (1999), which was designed by a team including architect Josep Lluís Canos and landscape architect Bet Figueras, takes species from the world's five Mediterranean climate regions and recreates the landscapes found in nature.

Other recent projects include the Aquileia Tower (2008), a residential and commercial project which reunites two previously disjointed piazzas in Venice; and the Roca Gallery in Barcelona (2009), an exhibition space and learning centre about the history of water, with a façade of blades of glass rhythmically illuminated by LED lights. West Beach Promenade in Benidorm, completed in 2010, recreates in white concrete the shapes of cliffs and waves with a series of convex and concave spaces full of light and shadow.

Carlos Ferrater was awarded the 2001 National Spanish Architecture Award and he has twice been a finalist for the Mies van der Rohe Award.

IMAGES: ALEJO BAGUÉ (TOP); OAB (RIGHT)

Benidorm waterfront

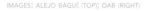

Sou Fujimoto
Japan

Sou Fujimoto's architectural design is ever in search of new forms and new spaces. After graduating in architecture from Tokyo University, his first built work was for Seidai Hospital for which he designed an occupational therapy building in 1996, adding a new ward in 1999. He founded Sou Fujimoto Architects in 2000. Much of his work continued to be in healthcare, particularly mental health. As with many young architects, he gained housing commissions: his T house (2005) with its radial walls creating a series of alcoves; the House at Tateyama (2007) with its limbs laid out to define specific views; and House N (2009), with its nest of boxes creating layers of privacy.

In 2005 he started to gain increased visibility, not least in the west, when he was highly commended for a residential care unit in Hokkaido in The Architectural Review Emerging Architects Awards. The following year he won the Grand Prize for his Treatment Centre for Mentally Disturbed Children, again in Hokkaido, taking yet a third Architectural Review award in 2007 with his house in Chiba. As a result he was invited to serve on the judging panel for the awards in 2008.

His first large-scale institutional project was the Musashino Art University Library which he describes as a forest of books. Although he had to simplify his competition-winning design, he has developed a spiral plan which allows for the linear as well as the random discovery of books.

His work was again celebrated by The Architectural Review in August 2011 when it published his project for an art museum in Aix-en-Provence: a series of buildings that exploit the functional, spatial and aesthetic potential of repetition, with a series of three cubic metre modules each set in a one square kilometre domain, containing one work of art.

IMAGES: D. VINTINER (TOP); SOU FUJIMOTO ARCHITECTS (RIGHT)

Musashino Art University Library

Anna Heringer
Germany

Anna Heringer was born in 1977 in Rosenheim, Germany, and studied at the University of Linz. She practices in Salzburg and also regularly in Bangladesh which she has visited annually since she did a voluntary year-out as development learner for social services in 1997.

In 2008 she developed the DESI building and HOMEmade project on rural housing in Bangladesh, running three months of workshops for architecture students from Bangladesh and Austria in cooperation with the non-governmental organisations Dipshikha and Shanti. The project won an Architectural Review Emerging Architecture Award. Between 2005 and 2006, working with Eike Roswag, she fundraised, organised, planned and implemented the METI handmade school project in Bangladesh, which won an Aga Khan Award for Architecture in 2007. The judges said: 'This joyous and elegant two-storey primary school in rural Bangladesh has emerged from a deep understanding of local materials and a heartfelt connection to the local community. Its innovation lies in the adaptation of traditional methods and materials of construction to create light-filled celebratory spaces as well as informal spaces for children.' The school also won an Emerging Architecture Award, from the Architectural Review in 2006.

She has been visiting professor at the University of Art and Design in Linz since 2008, during which time she has also held the Gertrud Luise Goldschmidt Professorship at the University of Stuttgart. She has acted as a consultant to the Aga Khan Foundation in Mozambique.

Her doctorate at the Technischen Universität Munich was entitled HOMEmade: practical strategies for sustainable building in the rural regions of northern Bangladesh making use of indigenous potential. She lectures in universities and at international conferences as well still getting her hands dirty helping to build the projects she has designed. She also finds time to illustrate children's books.

Meti

Christian Kerez
Switzerland

Christian Kerez's work is distinguished by constant formal and architectural research. He considers architecture to be the result of a continuing study of space and the pathways that lead through it. His preferred tools are models which he moulds and then constantly questions the results, incessantly exploring different design possibilities.

He was born in 1962 in Maracaibo, Venezuela, and in 1988 he graduated from the Swiss Federal Institute of Technology in Zurich where he has taught since 2001. He was a design architect in the office of Rudolf Fontana from 1991 to 1993. After extensive published work in the field of architectural photography, he opened his own architectural office in Zurich in 1993.

The Kunstmuseum in the Liechtenstein capital Vaduz (2000) was designed by Christian Kerez working with Meinrad Morger and Heinrich Degelo. The mysterious, highly tactile black box form is of tinted concrete and black basalt stone embedded with pebbles from the Rhine. Inside the black box becomes a white cube. Arranged around two staircases, the galleries have a precise clarity, while the plan enables diagonal views through the building.

Christian Kerez's 2003 Forsterstrasse apartment project is spread over five levels. The internal planning is reminiscent of Mies van der Rohe's brick wall houses: a series of orthogonal perpendicular walls defining individual spaces that flow from one to the other.

His 2007 Single Wall House in Zurich, an apparently simple project, is in fact sophisticated both structurally and spatially. It is two houses in a single structure where the volume is split both vertically and horizontally. The party wall zig-zags, adding to the interest by taking a different line on each of the three floors.

In the course of his career, Christian Kerez has exhibited all over the world, from New York to Paris and Shanghai.

IMAGES: KARIN HOFER (TOP); WALTER MAIR (RIGHT)

House with one wall

Francisco Mangado
Spain

Born in Navarre in 1957, Francisco Mangado gained a degree in architecture in 1982 from the University of Navarre School of Architecture. He combines his academic work at Navarre, Harvard, Yale and Lausanne with his architectural practice at his studio in Pamplona.

Francisco Mangado's award-winning work includes convention centres in Pamplona, Palenica and Navarre and a museum of archaeology Vitoria. His latest works are the extension of the Fine Arts Museum of Asturias in Oviedo; and an office tower in Buenos Aires. His works of urbanism include squares in Bordeaux, Olite, Estella and Madrid. His work is also recognised abroad. In Goa he has built a monastery, church and an aid centre, while in Japan he built a library for Kansai.

He was commissioned to design the Spanish Pavilion for the 2008 International Exposition in Zaragoza. The intricate ephemeral structure was composed of 750 clay columns with metallic cores, reminiscent both of a bamboo grove and a Graeco-Roman temple, which appeared to float in shallow pools of water. The clay drew up the water to cool the building – a gesture so beautiful and simple that visitors wondered why all eco solutions could not be like this. By contrast the Football Stadium in Palencia (2007) is simplicity itself: a straightforward ribbed metal box with four of the sturdiest yet most elegant pylons supporting floodlights ever seen in a sports arena.

The white cubes of his Municipal Exhibition and Congress Centre in Ávila (2009) form a dynamic contrast with the flowing drums of the honey-coloured city walls of the ancient town. Seen from the walls, the roof planes appear as a piece of sculpture hewn from the landscape. The Pamplona Congress Centre and the Ávila Congress Centre were shown at an exhibition on Spanish architecture held at MoMA in New York in 2006.

IMAGES: MANUEL COSTELLS (TOP); PEDRO PEGENAUTE (RIGHT)

Spanish pavillion 2008

THE RIBA HONORARY FELLOWSHIPS

In 2012 the RIBA awarded fourteen new
Honorary Fellowships to men and women
from a wide range of backgrounds, including
artists, writers, engineers, teachers, planners
politicians and those involved in the
administration of architecture.

RIBA Honorary Fellowships reward the
particular contributions made to architecture
in its broadest sense: its promotion,
administration and outreach; its role in
building more sustainable communities;
and finally its role in the education of future
generations. The lifetime honour allows
recipients to use the initials Hon FRIBA after
their name.

All these people, be they practitioners
or commentators, have done much for
architecture. In their very different ways, they
have all helped to improve the quality of
design and influence the delivery of the built
environment in a sustainable and creative
way.

This year's RIBA Honorary Fellows were
chosen by the Honours Committee, which
also selects the Royal Gold Medallist and
the RIBA International Fellows (see pages
182–189 and 190–196).

For the list of committee members, see
page 182.

Nicole Crockett
Director of Building Exploratory

Nicole Crockett is chief executive of the Building Exploratory where she provides strategic leadership to a team devising innovative education and lifelong learning opportunities for thousands of school children and hard to reach adults across East London. Her key motivation is to see more people involved in shaping their local area. Special projects bring communities, artists and built environment professionals together to creatively explore buildings and public spaces and take journeys of discovery into the design, development and transformation of some of London's best-loved places.

Throughout her career she has maintained a commitment to architecture, raising its profile amongst the wider population and promoting an agenda of inclusiveness. She worked as an Assistant Architecture Officer at Arts Council England when it was nurturing architecture and promoting the engagement of people with the design process. She then moved on to become Assistant Director of the Architecture Foundation for a four-year period. This allowed her to develop her ambition to see communities care for and inform change in the built environment. The desire to see architecture build its profile in a wider arts context, led to a key role at the Architecture Centre Network, which she chaired for three years between 2007 and 2009.

IMAGE: BUILDING EXPLORATORY

Robert Elwall
Photographs Curator
of the British Architectural Library, RIBA

Robert Elwall championed architectural photography for over 30 years. During his distinguished career as curator, author, critic, conservation advocate and lecturer, he built at RIBA the largest collection of architectural photography in the world – over 1.5 million images. Later he created a digital image database to disseminate its contents.

He curated dozens of ground-breaking exhibitions exploring the relationship between architecture, photography and society in libraries, museums and galleries both in London and beyond.

The author of a dozen monographs, Robert earned his reputation as an international authority in the field of architectural photography with his book Building With Light: the International History of Architectural Photography (2004).

Through both his writings and his talks Robert stimulated awareness of the value and the uses of architectural photography. He constantly strove to bring architectural photography to public attention, stressing its importance as a means of architectural and cultural expression and of enhancing of our sense of place.

His knowledge of and passion for architectural photography also helped to rescue countless photographic archives at risk, and his expertise to advocate better conservation and protection of buildings.

In March 2012 Robert sadly finally lost his long battle with cancer.

IMAGE: GABY HIGGS

Professor Adrian Forty
Professor of Architectural History,
The Bartlett School of Architecture,
University College London

Adrian Forty is an inspirational teacher. He is Professor of Architectural History at the Bartlett School of Architecture, UCL, where he has taught since 1973. After studying History at Oxford University, and Art History at the Courtauld Institute of Art, his career as an architectural historian began as the assistant to Reyner Banham at UCL. In 1980, with Mark Swenarton, he started England's first Master's programme in Architectural History which has made a major impact on the discipline, not least because Adrian has steered the understanding of architecture and its history in a more sociological direction.

He is also the Year 1 BSc History and Theory Coordinator, a course he has run since the early 1990s and refined so it provides a general introduction to the history of architecture and cities for all first year students. Keen that students should get away from the classroom he sets assignments which required them to investigate a wide range of buildings and art collections around London.

In his own scholarship his subjects are diverse, covering the architecture of Brazil, concrete, Fretton, memory, the primitive and Pevsner. As a result of his innovative approach to teaching he won the Sir Misha Black Award for Innovation in Design Education in 2003.

IMAGE: FRANCESSCA FORTY

Malcolm Hankey
Civic Trust Awards

Qualified as a Civil Engineer and with a degree in Law, Malcolm Hankey has a long-standing passion for architecture and believes strongly in the ethos of the Civic Trust Awards and its role in promoting excellence in design standards. The Civic Trust Awards together with RIBA members and their co-professionals have worked hand in hand over the last 52 years to deliver one of the longest standing architectural and environment awards schemes in Europe and one that is robust, highly respected and vital to promoting the industry. Awards are given to projects that demonstrate the highest standards of design, offer high sustainability and inclusive design credentials, whilst making a positive social, cultural, environmental or economic benefit to the local community. Malcolm believes that promoting excellent examples of inclusive architecture and design is vital to economic growth.

In 2009, The Civic Trust, as the parent charity, went into administration and Malcolm was instrumental in rescuing the Civic Trust Awards, which he runs on a not-for-profit basis, with the support of hundreds of volunteer assessors.

Previously Malcolm worked as an engineer with the National Rivers Authority and for the Environment Agency, involved in flood and coastal defence in the North West.

IMAGE: CIVIC TRUST AWARDS

Boris Johnson
Mayor of London

Former journalist and MP Boris Johnson has been a consistent champion of high-quality architecture in London and in particular of the way Londoners should be housed. Through the Greater London Authority he has introduced clear guidance to improve the design standards of new developments to ensure that homes have the space people need to live happy, healthy lives. Despite the urgent need to build many more homes in very difficult economic times, Boris Johnson has taken a clear stand on not compromising on quality. He has actively supported the RIBA's HomeWise campaign which will get households, architects, builders and policy makers involved in a conversation about how to deliver homes that meet – or exceed – what people need.

Under the Government's Localism Act the Mayor has acquired additional housing powers, taking responsibility for London's share of national housing budgets and for a portfolio of land and property assets. He has also taken a number of initiatives to improve the built environment in London, making it a better place for both Londoners and visitors. These include the creation of a £50m fund to boost regeneration and rejuvenate town centres at the heart of local London communities and the launch of The Mayor's Great Spaces initiative.

IMAGE: CITY HALL

Doug King
Environmental engineer

Doug King developed a taste for inter-disciplinary engineering design with Max Fordham and Buro Happold before setting up King Shaw Associates, a firm dedicated to what he terms 'building engineering physics'. As a short-hand this is building services integrated with structure, but that does not fully capture the way he has fused together the different aspects of engineering.

He has contributed to a number of ground-breaking sustainable buildings including two Stirling shortlisted schemes: Cullinan's Weald and Downland Gridshell and Chetwood Associates Sainsbury's Greenwich Supermarket, which Building magazine described as the most significant in the history of retailing; as well as the RIBA Award-winning Rolls Royce Factory at Goodwood by Grimshaw and Behnisch's RIBA International Award-winning Genzyme Centre in Cambridge, Massachusetts.

Doug's enthusiasm and drive to share his ideas led to his invitation to become a Royal Academy of Engineering Visiting Professor of Building Physics at the University of Bath. He also writes on environmental issues in construction, is a member of the RIBA Validation Panel, an advisor to The Ove Arup Foundation and a member of the South West Design Review Panel. He was awarded the Royal Academy of Engineering Silver Medal in 2011 for an outstanding personal contribution to British engineering.

IMAGE: ALEX KING

Fiona MacCarthy OBE
Writer

Fiona MacCarthy is a British biographer and cultural historian best known for her studies of nineteenth- and twentieth-century arts, crafts and design. She writes with exemplary insight on the place of architecture in our culture as a whole.

Her arts essays, reviews and columns have appeared regularly in The Guardian, the Times Literary Supplement and The New York Review of Books. She contributes frequently to TV and radio arts programmes. But she is most respected for her authoritative yet racy biographies of a number of key nineteenth- and twentieth-century artists and designers, including Byron, Edward Burne-Jones, William Morris, Charles Robert Ashbee, Eric Gill and Stanley Spencer. Her latest subject is architect Walter Gropius, who she met when he came to London for the Bauhaus exhibition in 1968.

She is the newly installed President of the Twentieth Century Society, the organisation concerned with the preservation and promotion of the best examples of twentieth-century architecture.

She and her late husband, the designer David Mellor, commissioned the RIBA Award-winning cutlery factory, The Round Building at Hathersage in Derbyshire, from their friend Sir Michael Hopkins. Fiona contributed much to the design studio, the factory and retail operations of the firm.

Frank McDonald
Environment Editor, The Irish Times

A watchdog for architecture and a whistleblower on poor development, Frank McDonald was born in Dublin in 1950 and lived until recently in Temple Bar, an area of the city he helped to save. Frank was one of those who protested about the destruction of Georgian Dublin in the late 1960s and '70s and he remains an outspoken critic of unsympathetic redevelopment but a vociferous supporter of good architecture, as well as a professional worrier about the environment. He is Environment Editor of The Irish Times, author of several books including *The Destruction of Dublin* (1985), *Saving the City* (1989) and *The Construction of Dublin* (2000) and joint author with Kathy Sheridan of *The Builders* (2008), which took a critical look at the developers involved in the so-called Celtic Tiger's casino culture.

He has reported on UN climate change conferences since 1995, including Copenhagen, Cancún and Durban and he is an articulate regular contributor to radio and television programmes. But Frank is first and foremost a newspaper man: he is always on the look-out for wrong-doing and knows how to use his talents to lead public opinion in order to help put things right.

Dr Sandra O'Connell

Architectural writer, editor and curator

Born in Ulm, Germany and educated at Trinity College Dublin, Sandra O'Connell is an architectural writer, editor and curator. She lives with her family in Dublin, Ireland and contributes in multiple roles to architecture and its importance to all our lives – a topic she feels passionate about.

Sandra regularly writes on Irish architecture and Modernism in particular, two interests close to her heart, and contributes to national and international conferences. She is editor of the RIAI's *Annual Review, Irish Architecture 2011/12*, a comprehensive edition of award-winning projects drawn from the RIAI's prestigious Irish Architecture Awards. Since 2002, she has been editor of *Architecture Ireland*, published by the Royal Institute of the Architects of Ireland (RIAI).

Inspired by Open House London, Sandra was founding curator of the first Open House Dublin event, which she continues to run on an annual basis for the Irish Architecture Foundation. She has made Open House Dublin Ireland's largest and most popular architectural event. Sandra is also a board member of darc space (Dublin Architecture Space), the only dedicated architecture gallery in the Republic of Ireland which aims to promote innovative energy-efficient and sustainable architecture.

IMAGE: EUGENE LANGAN

Peter Rees

Chief Planning Officer, City of London

As Chief Planning Officer of the City of London, Peter Rees's enthusiasm for his very special patch, the Square Mile, is palpable and derives from childhood visits to stay with an aunt. He studied architecture and planning at London's Polytechnic of the South Bank and his first Polytechnic assignment in 1968 involved sorting out Paternoster Square, something he had to do for real in his later professional life. He has seen it as a crucial part of his custody of the City, not only to ensure that business does not abandon it for Docklands or Frankfurt, but that it does not die by night or at weekends. For that reason he championed Jean Nouvel's One New Change Scheme and New Court, Rothschild's London headquarters, both shortlisted for the RIBA Stirling Prize.

His planning career has spanned periods with the Historic Buildings Division of the Greater London Council; private practice with Gordon Cullen; a spell at the Department of the Environment; and another as Assistant Chief Planning Officer to the London Borough of Lambeth.

He lectures at universities and conferences throughout the world and makes frequent media appearances covering a wide range of planning and urban design topics.

Professor Peter Salter
Teacher and Designer

Richard Simmons
Planner and former CEO CABE

Peter Salter is one of the most influential architectural teachers of the past 30 years. He talks, writes and draws with equal facility: he is a superb draftsman. A past employee of Alison and Peter Smithson, his teaching built directly on their legacy, leading another generation of students to appreciate the poetic capacities of construction. Architects such as Caruso St John and Sauerbruch Hutton have spoken of his formative influence on their way of working.

Peter is currently Professor of Architectural Design at the Welsh School of Architecture in Cardiff where he was appointed in 2006. Peter's teaching career began in the 1980s when he joined the AA School of Architecture as a technical tutor in the diploma school. In 1995 he was appointed successor to Ron Herron as Head of School and Professor of Architecture at the University of East London. His focus here was to develop a school with a specialism in exploring architecture through construction, with an emphasis on materials, as a way of engaging with issues of sustainability and low-energy construction.

In 2004 Salter won the Royal Institute of British Architects Annie Spink award for his outstanding contribution to architectural education. This prize was awarded jointly with Wolf Prix.

IMAGE: SANDRA MORRIS

Planner Richard Simmons was chief executive of the Commission for Architecture and the Built Environment (CABE) the government's adviser on architecture, urban design and public space from June 2004 until its merger with the Design Council in 2011. He is currently Visiting Professor of City Design and Regeneration in the School of Architecture and Construction, at the University of Greenwich. He is also an independent consultant and educator in urban design, planning, regeneration and public space.

As head of CABE, Richard was determined the organisation should be the government's watchdog not its lapdog when it came to architecture. A previous local authority and Whitehall man he had plenty of knowledge of that side of the planning equation, but he has a wealth of experience too as the developer's champion through his regeneration work in Kent and the east end of London.

Richard was a consistent advocate of the public and commercial value of good design, of using architects to produce high quality buildings and places, and of sustainable and inclusive design. Richard played a key role in CABE's contribution to the design of London 2012, and in conceiving and implementing the merger with the Design Council.

Chris Smith
English Heritage National Planning Director

Ai Weiwei
Artist

Chris Smith has been an historic environment management professional since 1974, working with local authorities and a Community Development Trust. He was awarded an OBE for his work in establishing the Institute of Historic Building Conservation. At English Heritage he oversees the expert statutory advisors in the planning and development field and co-ordinates the work of the Urban Panel which undertakes reviews of major urban issues.

While studying for a degree in Swedish literature at the University of East Anglia in Norwich – in one of Denys Lasdun's masterpieces – his eyes were opened to the richness of Britain's past as exemplified by a fine mediaeval city. Urban conservation and archaeology were taking great steps forward as professions at that time and he decided to dedicate his life to those disciplines.

He strongly believes that the historic environment can be re-used for the benefit of society through close engagement with the architectural profession and that great design depends on a profound understanding of context, without which there can be no meaningful dialogue between the existing and the new; conversely, where a complex context is understood and embraced, his view is that it can provide the starting point for modern buildings of true excellence.

Considered to be one of the most significant cultural figures of his generation in China and internationally, Ai Weiwei co-inhabits the roles of a conceptual artist, architect, curator, designer, photographer, film-maker, publisher and activist. Ai is admired equally for his art and his principles.

Ai's work has been seen in London. His *Sunflower Seeds* installation at Tate Modern Turbine Hall was made up of millions of small works, each one an intricately hand-crafted life-sized porcelain sunflower seed; the Lisson Gallery displayed 13 of his works including *Colored Vases*; and Somerset House presented his first outdoor public sculpture *Circle of Animals/Zodiac Heads*.

A perfectionist, he attracts a highly skilled and devoted staff at his studio, FAKE Design, from which he catapulted to international fame in the run-up to the 2008 Olympic Games, when he was design consultant for the Beijing National Stadium in collaboration with Herzog & de Meuron. During the process he decided to have his name removed from the project, nonetheless the Bird's Nest, as it was dubbed by the world press, is still very much an Ai Weiwei inspired project. Ai collaborated for a second time with Herzog & de Meuron on the Serpentine Gallery's Summer Pavilion in London in 2012.

IMAGE: GAO YUAN

THE RIBA PRESIDENT'S MEDALS STUDENT AWARDS

The RIBA President's Medals Student Awards are the RIBA's oldest award (pre-dating the Royal Gold Medal, which was formally established in 1848).

The RIBA awarded the Silver Medal for the first time in 1836 for the best architectural essay (and from 1855 for the best 'Measured Drawings' produced by a talented graduate). In 1984, the Institute created a Bronze Medal to reward the work produced by a Part 1 student and a Silver Medal to be awarded to a Part 2 student. In 2001 a Dissertation Medal was added. Since its early days, the aim of the awards has been to promote excellence in the study of architecture, to reward talent and to encourage architectural debate worldwide.

In 2011, the RIBA invited 300 schools of architecture in 60 countries to take part in the President's Medals. This was the highest number of schools invited in the history of the awards and generated the greatest ever number of entries.

The judging panel for the Bronze and Silver Medals was:
- Oliver Richards (Chair), RIBA Vice-President Education & architect, ORMS Architecture Design
- Jorge Ayala, architect, [AY]A Studio
- Alison Brooks, architect, Alison Brooks Architects
- Edouard François Int FRIBA, architect, Edouard François Architectes

The Dissertation Medal judging panel included:
- Professor Peter Blundell Jones (Chair), Professor of Architecture, University of Sheffield
- Professor David Edgerton, Hans Rausing Professor, Imperial College London
- Dr Alexandra Stara, Director of Graduate History and Theory and of the MA Thinking Building, Kingston University
- Dr Teresa Stoppani, Reader in Architecture, University of Greenwich

An exhibition of student work submitted for the 2011 awards was on display at the RIBA Headquarters in London between early December 2011 and late January 2012 before travelling throughout the UK and internationally.

The awards website (www.presidentsmedals. com), which forms a comprehensive archive of student talent comprising tens of thousands of images since 1998, remains very popular amongst students of architecture and the public.

HOUSING LONDONS - ROBOT WORKFORCE

Southwhyck House - On the prolific Moorlands estate on Coldhabour lane, readapted for London new robot workforce.

Electric Avenue has also being adapted with robots homes being extended on top of the existing Victorian terraces.

Throughout the year i explored ideas about the relationship between class and race with identity. I used Brixton, (or an augmented Brixton) as the stage for my exploration and represented my thoughts, ideas and development through prose, drawings, film, animation and the moving image.

I negatively criticised how society treats race, class and identity and how this has changed throughout my life time. Using Henry Lefebvre ideas of perceived and conceived space as a starting point, I developed complex spatial narratives to explore the idea of 'Spatial Justice'. Robots of Brixton draws parralells with the 1981 Brixton riots and shoes how prevalent they are today. It shows the architectural and spatial implications can be a major factors in causing portions of society to rise up and revolt.

These are a collection of images of what Brixton could be like if it were to develop as a disregarded area inhabited by London's new robot workforce. Built and design to do all the task humans no longer want to do. The population of brixton has rocketed and unplanned cheap quick additions have been made to the skyline.

SITE PLAN & SHOOTING SCHEDULE

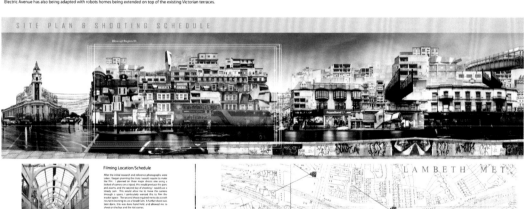

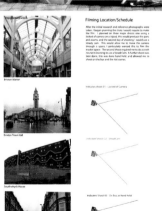

Filming Location/Schedule

After the initial research and reference photographs were taken, I began planning the shots i would require to make the film. I planned on three major shoots one using a lockout of camera on a tripod. this would produce the pans and zooms, and the second day of shooting i would use a steady cam. This would allow me to move the camera through a space. I particularly wanted this to film the market space. The second shoot required me to do a crash course in learning to use a Steadi-Cam. A further shoot was later done, this was done hand held, and allowed me to shoot on the bus and the riot scenes.

Robots of Brixton

STUDENT STATEMENT BY KIBWE TAVARES, BARTLETT SCHOOL OF ARCHITECTURE, UCL

Robots of Brixton is an architectural film project that explores the relationship between architecture, class and race. With Brixton (or an augmented Brixton) as its backdrop, the project uses robots as metaphors for a future intake of migrants to the UK. It acts as a commentary on the cyclical nature of the working class in areas with diverse populations.

The projects show Brixton as a degenerated and disregarded area inhabited by London's new robot workforce. The robots are built and designed to carry out all of the tasks which humans are no longer inclined to do. The mechanical population of Brixton has rocketed, resulting in unplanned, cheap and quick additions to the skyline.

The film follows the trials and tribulations of young robots surviving at the sharp end of inner city life, living the predictable existence of a populous hemmed in by poverty, disillusionment and mass unemployment. When the Police invade the one space which the robots can call their own, the fierce and strained relationship between the two sides explodes into an outbreak of violence echoing that of 1981.

Architecturally Robots of Brixton has three main design strands.

1. Urbanism and Masterplanning. To design the film I first had to readapt the architecture of Brixton. Social housing, markets, public buildings and spaces were all researched and redesigned at urban scale.
2. Film Design. The film in itself was a complex design project, all the environments, set design, transitions between films scenes all had to fit together harmoniously.
3. Robot Design. Using 2D and 3D techniques each robot was designed in detail.

Robots of Brixton is a project that bridges architecture and politics using the medium of film as an open and accessible way in. The England riots of 2011 amplify the subject matter as both potent and relevant.

http://www.vimeo.com/25092596

Street level Electric Avenue

The street level of electric avenue was also adapted. The beauty shop which sits at number 11 was replaced with a robot barber, named 'robo cuts'. I chose barber because the barbershop is a very important social space for the black community.

The street level of electric avenue was also adapted. The beauty shop which sits at number 11 was replaced with a robot barber, named 'robo cuts'. I chose barber because the barbershop is a very important social space for the black community.

SEQUENCE TWO - THE "CHARGE" HOUSE

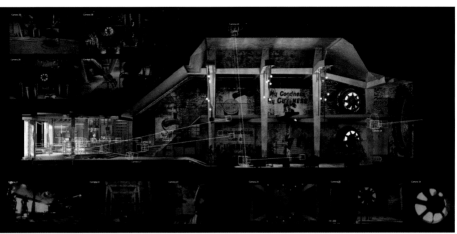

SEQUENCE THREE - THE DREAM SPACE

The third sequence in the film, is not a real space but a space in the mind of the Robot. In a sense the space is meant to be a utopia the robots cab go to escape the trial of everyday life. It is proportioned and based of cathedral like spaces this references the heightened importance of the church to migrant populations in the UK. The space is very important to the robots as its the only place they can call their own.

The sequence is important in the narrative as it is the space in which the film switches from being about a day in the life of this robot to an extraordinary day in the life of the robot. As the police robots enter the space you see that something foreign enters their space, the robots see this as an invasion and begin to riot. As the space collapses this draws parallels with what is happening in the real world, as well as the robots dream collapses. It is important to note that the main character looses all his scars and rust when in this utopian space.

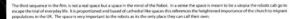

Plan and elevation of the dream space collapsing.

Plan and elevation of the dream space collapsing.

An Acoustic Lyrical Mechanism

STUDENT STATEMENT BY BASMAH KAKI,
ARCHITECURAL ASSOCIATION

This project speculates on sound energy and ambient space within the extreme setting of an active granite quarry. Located on the outskirts of the high-tech city Bangalore, the Silicon Valley of India, the mine employs a migrating cast – among them women and children – whose hearing is progressively damaged by the noise pollution endemic to their working conditions. An Acoustic Lyrical Mechanism creates a long-term strategy where sound and religious spaces offer relief, treatment and hope for the community of workers.

Inside the rock face, to protect against the mine's constant hammering sounds and blast vibrations, is an existing temple. It offers an entry point that then channels into a retreat space situated 30 metres above the quarry's floor, high enough to escape the destructive noises and yet embedded enough to listen to the sounds generated by a layered adaptive skin mechanism attached to the cliff rock.

The design was structured, firstly, around several prototypes, built to investigate Aeolian wind-belt harp concepts, and the conversion of kinetic energy into electrical and sound energy. Secondly, topographic models helped to analyse wind and natural updraft on steep surfaces and control the air/sound flow within the building. Wind catchers are positioned in order to amplify the prevailing wind, redirecting the updraft to play the building's instrumental spaces.

Operating as a sensorial extension of the existing temple, the building engages its users in educational programmes via lyrical mechanisms, tuning tools and sonic workshops. Crafted with the detail typically afforded to the manufacture of musical instruments, its internal spaces sit in contrast to its rough external setting. Like an Aeolian harp, the building is played by the wind, acoustically transforming the abrasive sounds of quarrying.

Part documentary, part speculation, the project reflects on sites and people lost in the rush of technological progress, but at the same time celebrating the cultivation of hope through acoustic lyrical mechanisms.

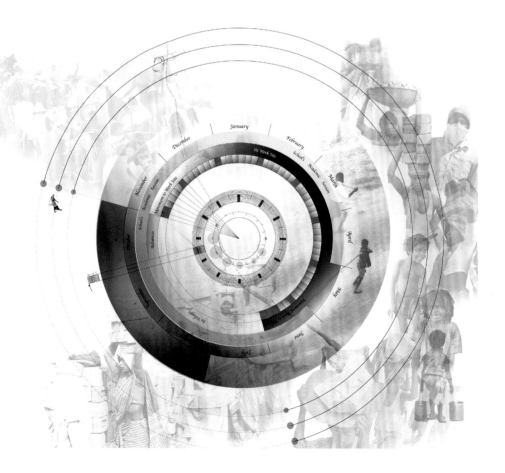

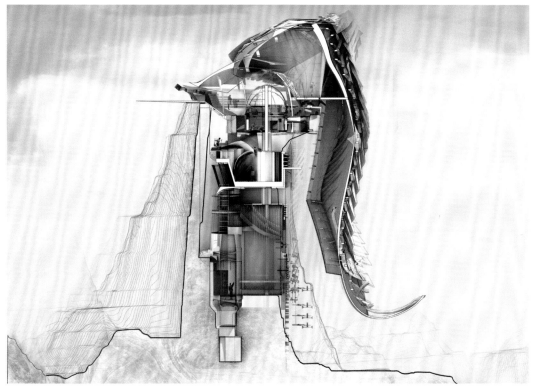

Bush Owner Builder

STUDENT STATEMENT BY HANNAH ROBERTSON, UNIVERSITY OF MELBOURNE

How do we develop culturally sensitive and appropriate housing for a remote Aboriginal community in Australia? I believe the answers are as diverse as the Aboriginal peoples themselves. This project promotes one option for specific application to one community, Hope Vale.

In the remote indigenous community of Hope Vale, southern Cape York in far north Queensland, the majority of housing is government-supplied. A substantial number of these houses are maltreated. There are maintenance problems, overcrowding and spaces not used for their intended purposes. This is partly owing to an attitude common among occupants that they are living in a council home instead of their own place.

Fundamentally, homelands refer to the traditional lands of an indigenous Australian group. Homelands hold incalculable spiritual and visceral significance to Aboriginal people, as elucidated by Hope Vale resident Victor Gibson: 'It just feels comfortable when you're in an area that belongs to you. It's the land of milk and honey.'

A shift to homeland living could alleviate the current situation in communities, however we need appropriate housing design solutions. Thus I have developed two homeland house designs using separate design methods. The first design was developed entirely from physical observations of the existing self-built shacks. In contrast, the second design has evolved from an extensive, hands-on consultative process with a local Hope Vale family. I then assessed the relative successes and failures of each approach by way of comparative analysis.

Both designs are being built as part of the Bush Owner Builder project, established in collaboration with Aboriginal leader Noel Pearson's Cape York Partnerships.

The success of this project will only be truly measureable once the houses have been constructed and occupied for some time. Then, perhaps this model could be replicated, but tailored accordingly, to suit other indigenous communities around Australia, taking into account the richness and diversity of cultural practices and issues.

PREVIOUS WINNERS *and*
ROYAL GOLD MEDALLISTS

The RIBA Stirling Prize

1996 Hodder Associates, University of Salford

1997 Michael Wilford and Partners, Music School, Stuttgart

1998 Foster + Partners, American Air Museum, Duxford

1999 Future Systems, NatWest Media Centre, Lord's, London

2000 Alsop & Störmer, Peckham Library and Media Centre, London

2001 Wilkinson Eyre Architects, Magna, Rotherham

2002 Wilkinson Eyre Architects, Millennium Bridge, Gateshead

2003 Herzog & de Meuron, Laban, London

2004 Foster + Partners, 30 St Mary Axe, London

2005 EMBT/RMJM, The Scottish Parliament, Edinburgh

2006 Richard Rogers Partnership with Estudio Lamela, New Area Terminal, Barajas Airport, Madrid

2007 David Chipperfield Architects, Museum of Modern Literature, Marbach am Neckar

2008 Feilden Clegg Bradley Studios, Alison Brooks Architects, Maccreanor Lavington, Accordia, Cambridge

2009 Rogers Stirk Harbour + Partners, Maggie's London

2010 Zaha Hadid Architects, MAXXI, Museo Nazionale delle Arti del XXI Secolo, Rome

2011 Zaha Hadid Architects, Evelyn Grace Academy, Brixton

The RIBA Lubetkin Prize

2006 Noero Wolff Architects, Red Location Museum of the People's Struggle, New Brighton, South Africa

2007 Grimshaw (Grimshaw Jackson Joint Venture), Southern Cross Station, Melbourne, Australia

2008 Gianni Botsford Architects, Casa Kike, Cahuita, Costa Rica

2009 Herzog & de Meuron, The National Stadium, Beijing

2010 Heatherwick Studio, UK Pavilion, Expo 2010 Shanghai, China

2011 WOHA with Tandem Architects The Met, Bangkok

The Adapt Trust Access Award

2001 Avery Associates Architects, Royal Academy of Dramatic Arts, London

2002 Malcolm Fraser Architects, Dance Base, Edinburgh

2003 Nicoll Russell Studios, The Space, Dundee College

The Architects' Journal First Building Award

2001   Walker Architecture, Cedar House, Logiealmond, Scotland

2002   Sutherland Hussey Architects, Barnhouse, London

2003   dRMM, No. 1 Centaur Street, London

2004   Annalie Riches, Silvia Ullmayer and Barti Garibaldo, In Between, London

2005   Amin Taha Architects, Gazzano House, London

The Crown Estate Conservation Award

1998   Peter Inskip + Peter Jenkins, Temple of Concord and Victory, Stowe

1999   Foster + Partners, Reichstag, Berlin

2000   Foster + Partners, JC Decaux UK Headquarters, Brentford

2001   Rick Mather Architects, Dulwich Picture Gallery, London

2002   Richard Murphy Architects with Simpson Brown Architects, Stirling Tolbooth, Scotland

2003   LDN Architects, Newhailes House, Musselburgh, Scotland

2004   HOK International, King's Library at the British Museum, London

2005   Avanti Architects, Isokon (Lawn Road) Apartments, London

2006   Dixon Jones with Purcell Miller Tritton, the National Gallery East Wing and Central Portico, London

2007   Alec French Architects, SS Great Britain and Historic Dockyard, Bristol

2008   Alastair Lansley (for Union Railways), St Pancras International, London

2009   Union North, The Midland Hotel, Morecambe

2010   David Chipperfield Architects in collaboration with Julian Harrap, Neues Museum, Museuminsel, Berlin

The RIBA CABE Public Space Award

2008   Gustafson Porter, Old Market Square, Nottingham

2009   McDowell + Benedetti Architects, Castleford Bridge, Castleford

2010   AECOM Design + Planning, Pier Head and Canal Link, Georges Parade, Liverpool

The RIBA Client of the Year

1998   Roland Paoletti: new Jubilee line stations, London

1999   MCC: buildings at Lord's Cricket Ground, London

2000   Foreign & Commonwealth Office: embassies around the world

2001   Molendinar Park Housing Association, Glasgow: buildings by various Scottish architects

2002   Urban Splash: regeneration in Manchester and Liverpool

2003   City of Manchester: post-IRA-bomb projects

2004   Peabody Trust: RIBA Award-winning schemes

2005   Gateshead Council: art and architecture projects

2006   Royal Botanic Gardens: buildings at Kew and Wakehurst Place

2007   Derwent London: 28 Dorset Square, London

2008   Coin Street Community Builders: Coin Street Neighbourhood Centre, London

2009   Camden & Islington Community Solutions: Kentish Town Health Centre, London; Grosvenor: Liverpool One Masterplan; Kielder Partnership: Kielder Observatory, Northumberland; Maggie's: Maggie's London; Parabola Land: Kings Place, London; St Martin-in-the-Fields, London

2010   Hammerson: 60 Threadneedle Street, London; Twenty Bishops Square/St Botolph's Hall, London

2011   Royal Shakespeare Company for the Royal Shakespeare Theatre and Swan Theatres, Stratford-upon-Avon

The RIBA Inclusive Design Award

2004   Arup Associates, City of Manchester Stadium

2005   Foster + Partners, Sage, Gateshead

2006   Adjaye/Associates, Idea Store, Whitechapel, London

2007   Patel Taylor, Portland College New Learning Centre, Mansfield

The RIBA Manser Medal

2001   Cezary Bednarski, Merthyr Terrace, London

2002   Burd Haward Marston Architects, Brooke Coombes House, London

2003   Jamie Fobert Architects, Anderson House, London

2004   Mole Architects, Black House, Cambridgeshire

2005   Robert Dye Associates, Stealth House, London

2006   Knox Bhavan Architects, Holly Barn, Norfolk

2007   Alison Brooks Architects, The Salt House, St Lawrence Bay

2008   Rogers Stirk Harbour + Partners, Oxley Woods, Milton Keynes

2009   Pitman Tozer Architects, Gap House, London

2010   Acme, Hunsett Mill, Stalham, Norfolk

2011   Duggan Morris Architects, Hampstead Lane

The RIBA Sorrell Foundation Schools Award

2007   Building Design Partnership, Marlowe Academy, Ramsgate

2008   Allford Hall Monaghan Morris, Westminster Academy at the Naim Dangoor Centre, London

2009   Penoyre & Prasad, The Minster School, Southwell

2010   Architype, St Luke's Church of England Aided Primary School, Wolverhampton

The RIBA Sustainability Award

2000   Chetwood Associates, Sainsbury's, Greenwich, London

2001   Michael Hopkins and Partners, Jubilee Campus, University of Nottingham

2002   Cottrell + Vermeulen Architecture, Cardboard Building, Westborough Primary School, Westcliff-on-Sea

2003   Bill Dunster Architects, BedZED, Wallington

2004   Sarah Wigglesworth Architects, Stock Orchard Street, London

2005   Associated Architects, Cobtun House, Worcester

2006   Feilden Clegg Bradley Architects, Heelis, Swindon

2007   Architype, Upper Twyford Barns, Hereford

2008   Denton Corker Marshall, Manchester Civil Justice Centre

The Stephen Lawrence Prize

1998   Ian Ritchie Architects, Terrasson Cultural Greenhouse, France

1999   Munkenbeck + Marshall, Sculpture Gallery, Roche Court, near Salisbury

2000   Softroom Architects, Kielder Belvedere, Northumberland

2001   Richard Rose-Casemore, Hatherley Studio, Winchester

2002   Cottrell + Vermeulen Architecture, Cardboard Building, Westborough Primary School, Westcliff-on-Sea

2003   Gumuchdjian Architects, Think Tank, Skibbereen

2004   Simon Conder Associates, Vista, Dungeness

2005   Níall McLaughlin Architects, House at Clonakilty, County Cork

2006   Alison Brooks Architects, Wrap House, London

2007   David Sheppard Architects, Wooda, Crackington Haven

2008   John Pawson, The Sackler Crossing, Royal Botanic Gardens, Kew, Richmond

2009   Simon Conder Associates, El Ray, Dungeness

2010   Gumuchdjian Architects, Artists' House, London

2011   Coffey Architects, St Patrick's Catholic Primary School Library and Music Room

The Royal Gold Medallists

The Royal Gold Medal for the promotion of Architecture, instituted by Her Majesty Queen Victoria in 1848, is conferred annually by the Sovereign on some distinguished architect, or group of architects, for work of high merit, or on some distinguished person or group whose work has promoted either directly or indirectly the advancement of architecture.

1848	Charles Robert Cockerell RA
1849	Luigi Canina, Italy
1850	Sir Charles Barry, RA
1851	Thomas L Donaldson
1852	Leo von Klenze, Austria
1853	Sir Robert Smirke, RA
1854	Philip Hardwick, RA
1855	JI Hittorff, France
1856	Sir William Tite
1857	Owen Jones
1858	August Stuler, Germany
1859	Sir George Gilbert Scott, RA
1860	Sydney Smirke, RA
1861	JB Lesueur, France
1862	Rev Robert Willis
1863	Anthony Salvin
1864	E Viollet-le-Duc, France
1865	Sir James Pennethorne
1866	Sir M Digby Wyatt
1867	Charles Texier, France
1868	Sir Henry Layard
1869	CR Lepsius, Germany
1870	Benjamin Ferrey
1871	James Fergusson
1872	Baron von Schmidt, Austria
1873	Thomas Henry Wyatt
1874	George Edmund Street, RA
1875	Edmund Sharpe
1876	Joseph Louis Duc, France
1877	Charles Barry
1878	Alfred Waterhouse, RA
1879	Marquis de Vogue, France
1880	John L Pearson, RA
1881	George Godwin
1882	Baron von Ferstel, Austria
1883	Francis Cranmer Penrose
1884	William Butterfield
1885	H Schliemann, Germany
1886	Charles Garnier, France
1887	Ewan Christian

1888 Baron von Hansen, Austria	**1929** Victor Alexandre Frederic Laloux, France
1889 Sir Charles T Newton	**1930** Percy Scott Worthington, FSA
1890 John Gibson	**1931** Sir Edwin Cooper, RA
1891 Sir Arthur Blomfield, ARA	**1932** Dr Hendrik Petrus Berlage, Netherlands
1892 César Daly, France	**1933** Sir Charles Reed Peers, CBE, PPSA
1893 Richard Morris Hunt, USA	**1934** Henry Vaughan Lanchester, PPTPI
1894 Lord Leighton, RA	**1935** Willem Marinus Dudok, Netherlands
1895 James Brooks	**1936** Charles Henry Holden, MTPI
1896 Sir Ernest George, RA	**1937** Sir Raymond Unwin
1897 Dr PJH Cuypers, Netherlands	**1938** Professor Ivar Tengbom, Sweden
1898 George Aitchison, RA	**1939** Sir Percy Thomas, OBE, JP, MTPI
1899 George Frederick Bodley, RA	**1940** Charles Francis Annesley Voysey
1900 Professor Rodolfo Amadeo Lanciani, Italy	**1941** Frank Lloyd Wright, USA
1901 (Not awarded, owing to the death of Queen Victoria)	**1942** William Curtis Green, RA
1902 Thomas Edward Collcutt	**1943** Professor Sir Charles Herbert Reilly, OBE
1903 Charles F McKim, USA	**1944** Sir Edward Maufe, RA
1904 Auguste Choisy, France	**1945** Victor Vessnin, USSR
1905 Sir Aston Webb, PPRA	**1946** Professor Sir Patrick Abercrombie FSA, PPTPI, FILA
1906 Sir L Alma-Tadema, RA	**1947** Professor Sir Albert Edward Richardson, RA, FSA
1907 John Belcher, RA	**1948** Auguste Perret, France
1908 Honoré Daumet, France	**1949** Sir Howard Robertson, MC, ARA, SADG
1909 Sir Arthur John Evans, FRS, FSA	**1950** Eliel Saarinen, USA
1910 Sir Thomas Graham Jackson	**1951** Emanuel Vincent Harris, OBE, RA
1911 Wilhelm Dorpfeld, Germany	**1952** George Grey Wornum
1912 Basil Champneys	**1953** Le Corbusier (CE Jeanneret), France
1913 Sir Reginald Blomfield, RA, FSA	**1954** Sir Arthur George Stephenson, CMG, AMTPI, Australia
1914 Jean Louis Pascal, France	**1955** John Murray Easton
1915 Frank Darling, Canada	**1956** Dr Walter Adolf Georg Gropius, USA
1916 Sir Robert Rowand Anderson, FRIAS	**1957** Hugo Alvar Henrik Aalto, Finland
1917 Henri Paul Nenot, Membre de L'Institut, France	**1958** Robert Schofield Morris, FRAIC, Canada
1918 Ernest Newton, RA	**1959** Professor Ludwig Mies van der Rohe, USA
1919 Leonard Stokes	**1960** Professor Pier Luigi Nervi, Italy
1920 Charles Louis Girault, Membre de L'Institut, France	**1961** Lewis Mumford, USA
1921 Sir Edwin Landseer Lutyens, OM, KCIE, RA, FSA	**1962** Professor Sven Gottfried Markelius, Sweden
1922 Thomas Hastings, USA	**1963** The Lord Holford, ARA, PPTPI, FILA
1923 Sir John James Burnet, FRIAS, RA, RSA	**1964** E Maxwell Fry, CBE
1924 Not awarded	**1965** Professor Kenzo Tange, Japan
1925 Sir Giles Gilbert Scott, OM, DCL, RA	**1966** Ove Arup, CBE, MICE, MIStructE
1926 Professor Ragnar ¨Ostberg, Sweden	**1967** Sir Nikolaus Pevsner, CBE, FBA, FSA, HonARIBA
1927 Sir Herbert Baker, KCIE, RA	**1968** Dr Richard Buckminster Fuller, FRSA, HonAIA, USA
1928 Sir Guy Dawber, RA, FSA	**1969** Jack Antonio Coia, CBE, RSA, AMTPI, FRIAS

1970	Professor Sir Robert Matthew, CBE, ARSA, FRIAS		1992	Peter Rice, DIC(IC), MICE
1971	Hubert de Cronin Hastings		1993	Giancarlo de Carlo, Italy
1972	Louis I Kahn, USA		1994	Michael and Patricia Hopkins
1973	Sir Leslie Martin		1995	Colin Rowe, USA
1974	Powell & Moya		1996	Harry Seidler, Australia
1975	Michael Scott, Ireland		1997	Tadao Ando, Japan
1976	Sir John Summerson, CBE, FBA, FSA		1998	Oscar Niemeyer, Brazil
1977	Sir Denys Lasdun, CBE		1999	The City of Barcelona, Spain
1978	Jørn Utzon, Denmark		2000	Frank Gehry, USA
1979	The Office of Charles and Ray Eames, USA		2001	Jean Nouvel, France
1980	James Stirling		2002	Archigram
1981	Sir Philip Dowson, CBE		2003	Rafael Moneo, Spain
1982	Berthold Lubetkin		2004	Rem Koolhaas, The Netherlands
1983	Sir Norman Foster		2005	Frei Otto, Germany
1984	Charles Correa, India		2006	Toyo Ito, Japan
1985	Sir Richard Rogers		2007	Jacques Herzog and Pierre de Meuron, Switzerland
1986	Arata Isozaki, Japan		2008	Edward Cullinan CBE
1987	Ralph Erskine, CBE		2009	Álvaro Siza, Portugal
1988	Richard Meier, USA		2010	I. M. Pei
1989	Renzo Piano, Italy		2011	Sir David Chipperfield CBE
1990	Aldo van Eyck, Netherlands		2012	Herman Hertzberger, Netherlands
1991	Colin Stansfield Smith, CBE			

Please note that the above list includes honorific tiles at the time of the award and professional but not academic qualifications.

SPONSORS *and* SUPPORTERS

The RIBA is extremely grateful to all the sponsors and supporters who make the awards possible.

TheObserver

The Observer, media partner for the RIBA Stirling Prize, is the world's oldest Sunday newspaper and is celebrated around the world for its journalistic excellence, liberal values and vigorous campaigning across a wide range of issues. *The Observer New Review*, the cultural heart of the paper, is renowned for its diverse arts coverage and acclaimed team of critics, including architecture critic Rowan Moore. Rowan's recent columns include a critique of London under Boris Johnson, an interview with Frank Gehry and an appraisal of the Shard. John Mulholland, *Observer* editor says: 'The *Observer* is a dedicated champion of British architecture so we are thrilled to be partnering with the RIBA to showcase the wealth of design talent that exists in this country.' Rowan Moore says:' The RIBA Stirling Prize has done more than any other British award to raise public awareness and understanding of architecture, which is also the aim of *The Observer*'s architectural coverage. It's a great pairing.'

The *Architects' Journal* has supported the RIBA Stirling Prize for more than a decade, because we believe the architectural profession benefits from a single preeminent award for great design. We partner with the Stirling Prize for the same reason we support programmes such as Open House London, the RIBA Awards and Manser Medal – as an extension of our role as the leading voice of the architectural profession. Of the independent architectural press, we have the furthest reach in the industry. The *AJ* doesn't just report, it influences, and has done for over a hundred years, since our founding in 1895. The profession has changed a lot since then – design went digital over twenty years ago and London has become the hub for global architecture. The *AJ* has changed too: we are now a breaking news organisation, publishing daily on our website, weekly on the iPad and in print, and minute-to-minute in conversation with over 40,000 followers on Twitter and 9,000 members on LinkedIn. We are proud to support the most prestigious award in British architecture, and give our hearty congratulations to the architect of the project built or designed in Britain that has made the greatest contribution to the evolution of architecture in the past year.

The Marco Goldschmied Foundation continues its fifteen year-long support for the Stephen Lawrence Prize, established in memory of the murdered teenager who aspired to be an architect. The Foundation provides the £5000 prize money and finds a £10,000 Stephen Lawrence Scholarship at the Architectural Association in London.

The Bloxham Charitable Trust

The first Client of the Year was named in 1998. The award recognizes the role that good clients play in the delivery of fine architecture. The fifth winner, in 2002, was Urban Splash, for 'its commitment both to design and quality and the regeneration of Manchester and Liverpool'/ Urban Splash's co-founder Tom Bloxham now supports the award through the Bloxham Charitable Trust.

RIBA Award plaques are produced and donated by the Lead Sheet association (LSA). The LSA is the primary independent body involved in the promotion and development of the use of rolled-lead sheet. The LSA is proud to have been associated with the RIBA Awards since 1989.

The RIBA would like to thank all the RIBA Awards judges who gave of their time so freely and whose reports form the basis of much of the text of this book.

The RIBA also thanks the photographers who agreed to waive copyright fees for the reproduction of their work in connection with the RIBA's promotion of the awards. Photography/illustration credits are provided on page except for the following (reproduced courtesy of the copyright holders): p. 183 Luchtfotografie; p. 184 (top left) Sybolt Voeten, (bottom left) Patrick Fransen, (top right) Rob Hoekstra; p. 185 Hans van den Bogaard; p. 186 Herman Hertzberger; p. 187 (top) Willem Diepraam, (bottom) John Lewis Marshall; p. 188 (top) Kees Rutten, (middle) Herman van Doorn, (bottom) Johan van de keuken; p. 189 (top left) Ger van der Vlugt, (top right) Herman van Doorn, (middle right) Rob Hoekstra, (bottom) Herman Hertzberger. Cover images: Hufton + Crow.

INDEX